Karma
and
Devotion

Also by Dr David R. Hawkins

BOOKS

Book of Slides: The Complete Collection Presented at the 2002–2011 Lectures with Clarifications

Discovery of the Presence of God: Devotional Nonduality

The Ego Is Not the Real You: Wisdom to Transcend the Mind and Realize the Self

The Evolution of Consciousness: Navigating the Levels of Awareness and Unlocking Spiritual Potential

The Eye of the I: From Which Nothing Is Hidden

Healing and Recovery

I: Reality and Subjectivity

In the World, But Not of It: Transforming Everyday Experience into a Spiritual Path

The Highest Level of Enlightenment: Transcend the Levels of Consciousness for Total Self-Realization

Letting Go: The Pathway of Surrender

The Map of Consciousness Explained: A Proven Energy Scale to Actualize Your Ultimate Potential

Power vs. Force: The Hidden Determinants of Human Behavior

Reality, Spirituality and Modern Man

Spiritual Power and Integrity: Uncovering Spiritual Reality and Realizing Peace, Love and Divinity

Success Is for You: Using Heart-Centered Power Principles for Lasting Abundance and Fulfillment

Transcending the Levels of Consciousness: The Stairway to Enlightenment

Truth vs. Falsehood: How to Tell the Difference

The Wisdom of Dr. David R. Hawkins: Classic Teachings on the Spiritual Truth and Enlightenment

AUDIO PROGRAMMES

How to Surrender to God

Live Life as a Prayer

The Map of Consciousness Explained

Please visit:

Hay House UK: www.hayhouse.co.uk
Hay House USA: www.hayhouse.com®
Hay House Australia: www.hayhouse.com.au
Hay House India: www.hayhouse.co.in

Karma and Devotion

The Sacred Path to God Through the Heart

Dr David R. Hawkins

HAY HOUSE

Carlsbad, California • New York City
London • Sydney • New Delhi

Published in the United Kingdom by:
Hay House UK Ltd, 1st Floor, Crawford Corner,
91–93 Baker Street, London W1U 6QQ
Tel: +44 (0)20 3927 7290; www.hayhouse.co.uk

Text © David and Susan Hawkins Revocable Trust, 2025

Cover design: Julie Davison
Interior design: Lilly Penhall

The moral rights of the authors have been asserted.

All rights reserved. No part of this book may be reproduced by any mechanical, photographic or electronic process, or in the form of a phonographic recording; nor may it be stored in a retrieval system, transmitted or otherwise be copied for public or private use, other than for 'fair use' as brief quotations embodied in articles and reviews, without prior written permission of the publisher.

The information given in this book should not be treated as a substitute for professional medical advice; always consult a medical practitioner. Any use of information in this book is at the reader's discretion and risk. Neither the authors nor the publisher can be held responsible for any loss, claim or damage arising out of the use, or misuse, of the suggestions made, the failure to take medical advice or for any material on third-party websites.

The original talk titles for this lecture series, The Way to God, are *Devotion: The Way to God Through the Heart* and *Karma and the Afterlife*.

A catalogue record for this book is available from the British Library.

Tradepaper ISBN: 978-1-83782-213-3
E-book ISBN: 978-1-4019-7715-3

10 9 8 7 6 5 4 3 2 1

This product uses responsibly sourced papers, including recycled materials and materials from other controlled sources. For more information, see www.hayhouse.co.uk

The authorized representative in the EU for product safety and compliance is Penguin Random House Ireland, Morrison Chambers, 32 Nassau Street, Dublin D02 YH68, Ireland. https://eu-contact.penguin.ie

Printed and bound by CPI Group (UK) Ltd, Croydon CR0 4YY

Contents

The Map of Consciousness® vi
Introduction vii

CHAPTER 1: The Pathway of Love 1

CHAPTER 2: Fields of Consciousness 51

CHAPTER 3: The Significance of Karma 91

CHAPTER 4: A New Paradigm of Reality 119

Conclusion 167
About the Author 171

Map of Consciousness®

God-view	Life-view	Level		Log	Emotion	Process
Self	Is	Enlightenment	⇧	700-1000	Ineffable	Pure Consciousness
All-Being	Perfect	Peace	⇧	600	Bliss	Illumination
One	Complete	Joy	⇧	540	Serenity	Transfiguration
Loving	Benign	Love	⇧	500	Reverence	Revelation
Wise	Meaningful	Reason	⇧	400	Understanding	Abstraction
Merciful	Harmonious	Acceptance	⇧	350	Forgiveness	Transcendence
Inspiring	Hopeful	Willingness	⇧	310	Optimism	Intention
Enabling	Satisfactory	Neutrality	⇧	250	Trust	Release
Permitting	Feasible	Courage	⇕	200	Affirmation	Empowerment
Indifferent	Demanding	Pride	⇩	175	Scorn	Inflation
Vengeful	Antagonistic	Anger	⇩	150	Hate	Aggression
Denying	Disappointing	Desire	⇩	125	Craving	Enslavement
Punitive	Frightening	Fear	⇩	100	Anxiety	Withdrawal
Disdainful	Tragic	Grief	⇩	75	Regret	Despondency
Condemning	Hopeless	Apathy	⇩	50	Despair	Abdication
Vindictive	Evil	Guilt	⇩	30	Blame	Destruction
Despising	Miserable	Shame	⇩	20	Humiliation	Elimination

© The Institute for Spiritual Research, Inc., dba/ Veritas Publishing.
This chart cannot be reproduced.

Introduction

For many spiritual aspirants, dedicated to Truth and Awareness, realizing the consciousness level of Love is our intention and motivation. To be more caring, to be forgiving, to feel the Presence of God on a deeper level are qualities that can be a reality; and through direct experience each one of us can know that "Love is a Way of Being" as we live in the world, in our daily lives.

But, how do we walk the path of Love in our day-to-day lives? How do we let go of our judgments and resentments of others and be more compassionate to those who have hurt us, and who appear to be unkind and devoid of love? In this book, Dr. David R. Hawkins gives the insights, encouragement, guidance, and techniques to be just that: freer, more loving, and kind.

In the previous books transcribed from the 2002 lecture series, The Way to God, Dr. Hawkins presented the transformative information that showed us the blocks to Love. He focused on the importance of understanding the nature of the ego, how it is structured, the importance of recontextualizing it and how it can be transcended. By understanding the levels of consciousness, from the lowest to the highest, the capacity to transcend to higher levels can occur, which includes going beyond the Mind.

Dr. Hawkins, in this volume, takes a huge leap from the pathway of Mind and presents the Pathway of Love. He starts by saying: "Today we are going to talk about that which cannot be spoken about." This Pathway of Love is extraordinarily powerful, with the capability of sweeping all capacity to function aside. Love takes a thousand different forms, from the more personal to Enlightenment.

He also discusses karma, it's significance and meaning both personally and globally, and how it can help anyone on the path to Awakening. He says, "It has the capacity to light up areas of your own life so that they make sense."

In your hands is the fifth book of the six-book series which comprises the September and October 2002 lectures: Devotion: The Way to God through the Heart, and karma and the Afterlife.

Some of the topics discussed in this book are:

Part 1
The consciousness level of Love
Devotion: a Pathway of Love
Love through Beauty and Music
Love is everywhere present and is within you at all times
How to Let Go of attachments
Surrender the Blocks to Love
The Power of Forgiveness

Part 2
The True Significance of Karma
The opportunity to undo negative karma and gain positive Karma
Karma and Reincarnation are two different things
Knowing your "Karmic Inheritance" can bring great strides
   and freedom
Understanding Karma can bring healing and end confusion

***

These are just a few of the inspiring truths you will read about in this stirring volume.

After reading this book, we wish you greater understanding and a stronger purpose to live a Pathway of Love.

Susan Hawkins & the Veritas Staff

CHAPTER 1

The Pathway of Love

Today we're going to talk about that which cannot be spoken about. This is going to be an experiment. I don't give you any guarantee about what will happen today because I don't know myself. Today we're talking about the Pathway of Love, which is extraordinarily powerful and is quite capable of sweeping all capacity to function aside.

So, you're aware that everything is happening of its own, as an expression of Divinity, which is the Allness, the totality of all that exists—the realization that one's own existence is due to the constant presence of Divinity. Contrary to the unenlightened view that Divinity threw the dice somewhere back in history and then disappeared, and is waiting for you somewhere until that awesome day called "Judgment Day," is a terrifying misconception of reality.

It's because of the Presence of God right now. One's existence from instant to instant is dependent completely on the Presence of God. One could say that that which one considers to be one's self, the ego, is the content, and God is the ultimate context. So, self with a small *s* is the content. Self with a large *S* is the context. Enlightenment is merely identifying progressively with the infinite Self, realizing that one is All That Is, forever.

In the first lecture we said that (and in every lecture, we affirm that) one of the most important pieces of information to realize is that there is no such thing as "cause" in the world—that is an abstraction. That the whole basis of the ego is based on the premise of "cause." "Cause" is based on duality. "Cause" is the belief that there is a "this" causing a "that," separate in time and place.

If there has to be a "this" causing everything, then there has to be a "this" causing whatever you think you are. And that's how the ego maintains some semblance of belief. There must be an actor behind your actions; there must be a speaker behind your speaking. There's got to be a doer behind your doingness.

And therefore, the illusion that there is a "this" causing a "that" is the main block. It is also the whole basis of science.

I was looking at a book somebody sent me, putting together advanced quantum mechanics in brain function. And you see how linearity strains and strains and strains to reach that which is really nonlinear. The book calibrates at 465. Trying to push the concept of "cause" to its ultimate and make it fit a realm in which there is no "cause" is quite a difficult task.

Today is like a bird trying to describe to you what a bird is like. The only thing that can describe what a bird is like is a "not-bird." If you're not a bird, you can describe what a bird is like, but if you are a bird, what can you say about it? "I go from tree to tree and I eat worms." End of story, you know. You just are that which you are. And the realization of that can sometimes take you out of the world quite a bit.

* * *

So, we're talking about love. The first eight lectures were really preparatory. Because we can talk about the ego; we can describe it. First of all, transcending duality to nonduality involves quite a deal of learning in a way. And of course, we can let go of that learning when the state itself prevails. We tried to cover the main blocks to love as the ultimate realization by taking apart the ego, seeing how it's constructed, basically dualistic due to positionalities. These positionalities are due to common belief systems, which really arise originally from the animal kingdom. So, it's not necessary to feel guilty about so-called "having an ego" (in quotes), because we inherited it from worms and birds and other things, which are inherent in the brain.

See, as the animal evolves, as consciousness evolves, it first appears on the planet as animal. The animal is only interested in survival; it has to find its way around in a physical domain and it operates out of a "this" and a "that." If there is a worm there and you're a bird here, you've got to gauge the distance between here and the worm, and *whop!* You have to know direction, distance, timing. And the same mechanisms are still inherent in our brain. So, the origin of thinking dualistically is really within the animal domain. The origin of the feeling states, of the fields of consciousness, are also in the animal domain, huh? They all have to do with survival.

Wow, thank you, Lord! My functioning today is totally up to God because I have no capacity to function whatsoever today. I come from a total state of nonfunctioning, and therefore, whatever happens, I've got nothing to do with it. So, I will not take any blame for anything that happens here.

This is the most difficult lecture, and I don't know if we'll be able to do it or not, but we'll attempt it. So, today will be an experiment to see if one can be that which you are and also talk about it. The capacity to function in the world for many years by avoiding the world, was how I handled the world; by not going there and retiring to a small town. Then the capacity to function gradually returned by some kind of intention that came from elsewhere, and the capacity to function in the world even until now is occasioned by humor.

It was discovered that humor would allow you to relate to the world and still be in that inner state. And, therefore, my usual style socially has to do with humor because the world is an endless comedy in which everything gets converted to its opposite, totally confused and misrepresented, and much hullabaloo is made about that, see. In which cause and effect, perpetrator and victim are totally reversed, which I am describing in the book *I*, the impact of the Luciferic. It really is concerned about the impact of the satanic—war, rape, killing, murder, blood, and grime and stuff like that.

More subtle and more powerful really is Luciferic, which distorts and reverses things in such a way as to confuse reality so you can't see reality anymore.

The Luciferic—that opens the door to the satanic; that's how war comes about. First, you have to confuse the people as to who's the perpetrator and who's the victim, and that opens the door, and then through the door comes the satanic with its guns and its murder and its killing. But first you have to prepare the field with the Luciferic. The purpose of Luciferic is it is very profitable. That's why deep pockets are traditionally demonized in our society—eat too many hamburgers, it's their fault; they sold them to you, not "I'm overweight." I mean, you see the perpetrator and the victim, yeah?

The perpetrator is really the guy who eats too much, and the victim is really . . . and now we're going to turn it around, see. So, you see that happening all the time at war. You see that war is always preceded by the Luciferic distortion that, "Oh, those guys aren't that bad. We don't have to make any preparation for it; they aren't that bad." Yeah, right. They aren't that bad. That cost 70 million people in World War II, 70 million people. They aren't that bad—no, sir! Well, they were. So therefore, the world is an endless comedy, and if you can stay in the comedy of it, you can still be in a very good place within yourself and still function within the world.

The pathway of the heart, of course, is one of the great traditions. What we have been talking about up to now is primarily the pathways through nonduality. We've been talking in terms that are familiar to students of Zen and Buddhism and, traditionally, nonduality. The pathway of devotion through the heart takes the form of karma yoga, devoting all one's actions to God. And devotion in which Christianity probably is most prominent in the world today.

LOVE AND FORGIVENESS

Mother Teresa would be, let us say, an example of the unconditional love. There're many programs available to everyone: the 12-step programs, *A Course in Miracles* . . . these are all the pathways of love. The willingness to forgive and forget, let bygones be bygones. And then *A Course in Miracles* takes you even beyond that. So, the 12-step programs take you to unconditional love, which is the ultimate aim of Christianity, taught by Jesus Christ. To love your enemy as yourself, to forgive them. Unconditional love towards all that exists calibrates at 540.

Traditionally, if you get to Love, you don't have to worry, because as you leave the body, you will go to that which you are, which is lovingness and a heavenly state. How to arrive at those stages: so, the first lectures we gave were trying to take apart the obstructions to love so that, once you remove their underpinnings when they come up as an obstacle, they're much easier to let go of, because you realize that what you're talking about in these obstacles to love are always perceptions, how you perceive something. So, if we see how the ego puts together perception, we can disassemble it when that block comes up. And you realize, for instance, all the pathways of love talk about forgiveness, but forgiveness truly is not possible if you continue to see somebody as bad, evil, wicked, at fault. It's only when you can remove your own projections and your own perceptions and not label them as anything that you realize that basically they are innocent. That they don't know any better. So, that way you can stop hating them. You can forgive them for not knowing. So, forgiveness is not really possible until really to a certain degree you transcend dualistic perception, which labels everything as good and bad, deserving and undeserving, etc.

So, the doorway to Unconditional Lovingness is sort of the dawning on you that everything is innocent. Everything is innocent. Some are conscious; some are not conscious. That's the difference. Unconscious innocence will kill you in the name of Allah. And unconscious innocence will kill Islamics for Jesus. And I told you about the lifetime where we were both Crusaders and he was there for Allah and I was there for Jesus, and as we killed each other deader than a mackerel, we went out of body and both burst into hysteria. It was so funny; it was hysterical. I'll never forget it. I said, "Geez, I did it for Jesus." He said, "I did it for Allah."

Well, it was an important point. We both knew it, too, that we'd transcended a really max point of the evolution of consciousness. So, periodically throughout time, we've been buddies. You know, when I need somebody to kill me or I need somebody to kill, he volunteers, and we do each other in and transcend that level. So that's love of the highest kind. If it comes to reaching enlightenment, of course, you can't do it that way; you've got to give them a fierce fight, or it's not real. So, within this world, you see, all those things, to us, are very, very real. And if they are not very, very real, because if you realize it's a gameboard, it's not very real to you anymore, and you can't get the lesson out of it that you were seeking. You've got to actually be terrified of death in order to walk through death. Once you realize that it's a game, you can't do that anymore.

LOVE IS A WAY OF BEING

So, we're going to talk about love to the degree that we're able to talk about love today. And if love takes over, we may or may not continue to talk about love. In those states, it's best to have close friends around you. If you're really going into spiritual work seriously, it's advisable to have family, friends, be in an ashram, or at least have spiritual friends who are able to be of assistance should you become incapacitated, which is quite possible. And, sometimes, you don't know how you're going to get here, but your friends put you in a car, and they put coffee in your hand, and they drive you here, so that's how you get here; so, assistance appears magically, you know.

So we are going to talk about the various understandings of love. And the various reflections of love, because most people are more loving in more ways than they realize. They're unconscious of it. The other day I was polishing this chrome around the top of the stove, and it was clean, but not really shiny, so I took a steel wool and I started scrubbing it like that, and then it shone like that, and I said, "Now, you see, it shines with love." So, love takes many forms, doesn't it? Duty, commitment, caringness about everything, love for your body. You know, you've got to love this thing. And if you don't, your wife complains bitterly that you don't look nice, so if you fail it, somebody will remind you to feed it, and all the things that are necessary to go with it.

So, love takes many, many expressions. It takes the form of caringness. See, we look at love as some maybe advanced state, and "Oh, we're not there yet." No, that's not so. Love is constant in our life, see, because nobody is *completely* at one level or another, see. Let's say, well, this guy is at 125, so he can't know what the higher levels on the Map are like. No, certain aspects of him do. And those aspects show up in certain aspects of life. So, we begin to nurture those aspects and appreciate those aspects of life in which love is taking a form not easily labeled as love. See, in our world, love, you know, denotes romance, denotes here and there, denotes a "me" loving "you" and a "you" loving "me." And that kind of love can be lost. It can be won or gained or lost or taken away from you. So that's a different kind of love than spiritual love, which is awareness of a reality that is within you at all times. So, in reality, *love is a way of being in the world.* Love is actually a style, a way of being. It's a way of holding yourself in life and every aspect of life within an overall context. And that overall context gives it a different meaning and significance, a different appearance, huh? It is just as important to polish the chromium as it is to save the life of somebody dying by the side of the street, you understand? It's just that capacity takes this form here; it turns over the beetle that's on its back; here, it saves somebody that's bleeding by the side of the street and calls 911; and here, it helps you in the door so you can get through, you see what I'm saying? So, it's that capacity, that willingness to be that to the world.

One has no idea of how that is going to be expressed. It may be explaining something to somebody. It may be telling them how to get to 33rd and Fordham. You say, "How do you get to 33rd and Fordham from here?" You say, "You go here, and you go there,

KARMA AND DEVOTION

and—you can't get to 33rd and Fordham from here." You can't get to there from here, no.

So, we see that love takes a thousand different forms, often unrecognized as what it is. As one gets more spiritually committed and advanced, you know, you begin to recognize its expression, and you begin to see love everywhere. And, as you get into certain states, the beauty and perfection of all things and the constant presence of love become somewhat staggering. At that point, it may be somewhat difficult to function in the world, because everything reflects this beauty, and consequently, one has a tendency to break into tears. So, as you get into, let's say, the high 500s, there's a phase in which you cry all the time.

People think you're sad, and it's quite the opposite. It's because everything is so exquisitely beautiful that beauty and love are one and the same thing. That which is loving is beautiful, and that which is beautiful is an expression of love, because Divinity expresses itself in perfection. In the lower levels, one doesn't see perfection.

What does one see in the lower levels? One sees all your own projections. You constantly see that there's nothing worth anything in the world; you see that everything is sad. Here, you see everything as frightening. Here, you want everything. Here, you're mad about everything. Here, you're arrogant about everything. And then, you don't get to give the lecture until you get to Courage.

I said this morning, "We're going." No, she said this morning, "We're going." And here, if you get here or you don't, it's all the same.

Life doesn't depend on one thing or another. So, Neutrality you really reach by detaching from things.

So, orange kitty, to be dramatic, got jealous of this affair, and the day before, yesterday afternoon, disappeared. The whole staff, everybody, instead of preparing for the lecture, scattered all over the landscape looking for the kitty. And there was a big hole in the screen—that's how kitty got out—so, anyway, kitty was found, and the day was saved.

So, it was necessary to re-release on kitty. In other words, to let kitty go. And let go any attachment to kitty, and so, if kitty was found, it was wonderful, and if kitty was not found, it was okay. And so, we see those losses. What we look at as losses are all opportunities to let go of attachments. So, yesterday I had a chance to let go of any attachment that has developed over the years with kitty. So, if kitty was lost it was okay, and if kitty was found, it was very good.

So, we see that to move up, we move up to Willingness. The whole spiritual direction is based on Willingness. The willingness to let go of attachments such as I did with kitty yesterday, just to make sure I wasn't attached to kitty. The willingness to make the sacrifices that are necessary. The willingness to apply that which you've learned. So, all spiritual direction, then, depends on a certain willingness.

And probably the most important Willingness is the willingness to surrender things to God. Some people say, "Willingness about what?" The willingness to surrender things because the obstacles to love are all attachments to that which is unloving, and the willingness to surrender them and let go of the attachment.

RENUNCIATION: LETTING GO OF WORLDLINESS

So, the pathway of devotion, then, is a willingness to constantly surrender anything and everything. It becomes extreme, the willingness to sacrifice all one's positions, titles, money. Let go of all that this world has to offer—limousines and estates and titles and membership in great societies, etc., and walk away from all of it, hmm. So, that is a classic stage in spiritual development. What do we call it where you let go of everything in the world and want to walk away from it? Renunciation. So, we then come to Willingness that will eventually take you to renunciation. Renunciation takes the form, classically, in some pathways as literally renouncing the world. Literally walking away from the world. Moving out to the middle of nowhere and living on a cot with a box, a candle, and trucking manure—at 40 bucks a truckload—that's hysterical. And, anyway, it can take the form of the willingness to renounce everything. And most people who have been at spiritual work for some time have usually let everything go several times.

You walk away from it all, start from zilch, and as time goes on, it begins to accumulate around you again, and so then you go through another big letting go. Sometimes, like right now, because I'm writing, and I'd like certain references that I vaguely remember from somewhere in time. But usually, book readers who live in the 400s want references in the back with page numbers and stuff, you know. You can't just tell them. *How to Know God: The Yoga Aphorisms of Patanjali*, or something like that, they want to know, published by whom, what page? Anyway, they're missing the whole point of it. If you get the point of it, you don't look at any references, but anyway.

So, renunciation, then, can take the form of walking away from everything. I threw out my whole spiritual library—walked away from it all. Walked away from my medical library, walked away from all those things, and now, when I need a reference, I have to have someone look it up on the Internet. I remember what it's about, and it's just a point I want to make in a reference, but now they expect it in a reference.

So, having let go of one's spiritual library, all one's pictures of Jesus and all that stuff, you know, you walk away from all that because it's trappings. It's all trappings—incense and sandals and pictures of Jesus and Buddhas and all that stuff. Throw them all out. They're just pictures; they're just depictions; they're not the real thing, you know what I'm saying? So, you walk away from it, and you feel clean and pure and wonderful, but then you've got to have something to drive around in, so then you get a car, then you have to have a garage for the car. Unless you want to go shopping every day, you've got to have a refrigerator, so all this stuff begins to accumulate again. And you say, I don't know how I'm going to do this world, because, you know, you forgot you've got this thing here, a body, and it's entertaining, but it has certain needs. Like the kitty, you've got to give it food in the morning—I feed the kitty and I feed this body. I have my coffee, kitty has the food, so we're both happy. If you don't do that, it falls over. You get weak. Sometimes I say to Susan, "God, I'm so weak, I can't even walk from here to there." She says, "Well, if you eat something, that will help." I still find it hard to believe that you have to eat something, and I really don't. On days like today I just live on liquids and food—it's horrible.

So, renunciation, then, means letting go of worldliness, craving, wanting. So, you're trying to transcend the solar plexus. Wanting things is coming out of the solar plexus. "I want this, I want that." I mean Walmart is the cathedral of wantingness.

I love Walmarts! I always talk about Walmarts because it's our new cathedral. There's a certain Divinity there. It's God expressed as everything you could want. God says, "You want all these things; here they are!" Walmart is a present from God through the solar plexus of humanity. And not just the solar plexus, but you've got to keep this thing going, which means you gotta wash it, you gotta get soap, you gotta get things to put the soap in. You have to have refrigerators, all that stuff, so Walmart is very helpful for survival. I always speak well of its founder, Sam.

So, renunciation then takes the form of letting go of what the world chases after. Success, money, power—these are very important. See, the things that you do at what you consider beginning levels of spirituality—oh no, they're not "beginning." That's the test at the end. At the last lecture, we're going to give you what the test is like at the end.

The test at the end had been learned early in the game. I had let go of any desire for power. Somebody would say, "You want power?" I'd say, "What for?" It's a drag. You try being president of the United States or the pope, man. If you live 24 hours, it's because of the security around you; I mean, you know? There's nothing worse than having power. So, when that temptation comes at the end, you've refused it years before. You laugh at the Luciferic temptation: "All power is yours. Claim it." What are you, a joker? Lucifer's best shot. So, those things that will come to you later under a different form, they are profoundly powerful as they come. When you get very, very advanced, these things are going to come back to you.

So, these lessons we learn here are powerfully important. If you can let go of the kitty, you can let go of anything. After I let go of kitty, kitty of course, reappeared. Found by friends and people we work with and love. So, renunciation is really an inner . . . see, when you renounce the world, that's a "put it where your mouth is." Put your dukes up, and let's see if you're just saying that or if you really mean it. Can you really walk away from it all?

And when I first came to Sedona, most waiters and people around here were people who had done that. This was a mecca for the spiritually inspired, and the population was three or four thousand. Most of the waiters and staff in restaurants had once been president of so-and-so corporation. So then it was full of people who had once been wealthy and powerful and had all kinds of titles and said, "To hell with it." And now they walked around in sandals and long hair and went, "Om," all day. And their family thought they'd gone nuts, and "you'd better see a doctor." So, the spiritual madness can take you over, and you walk away from everything, and I've done it a couple of times, walked away from it all.

Then it comes to you in its more pristine understanding that renunciation is an internal affair. Renunciation means the willingness to surrender within yourself, your cherished positionalities, and more importantly, to surrender the juice you get out of these positionalities. The reason you can't transcend the ego is because you get such wonderful juice out of it. Being mad, being angry, being furious, being right, being just.

You watch the Middle East, the glee with which they kill each other. I mean, they love it, you know what I mean? Like an idiot, you're going to go over there with a peace thing. The first thing they'll do is kill you. Any idiot who goes over there with peace is going to ruin the whole game. There isn't a single person there that is interested in peace, except the peace-mongers, who get all their publicity and power from selling everybody peace. Hmm, yeah, right. Kill them peace-ers; man, they ruin their business. I mean, the whole racket is based on anything but peace, and you want to come in and blow their whole racket.

Like asking Dillinger to give up crime. I mean, what would he do without robbing banks? You know what I'm saying? Robbing banks is Dillinger's whole thing, right? After these miraculous escapes, what does he do? Within 48 hours he's out robbing a bank. Also, these bank robbers—what did he do with the last money he had? Three days ago, they got $48,000; two days ago, they got $14,000. I mean, did he spend it all, or what? Is he broke? No. Robbing banks is what he does; that's who he is; that's his thing, you know. So, you can hold a parade that says, "Stop robbing banks." Yeah, right.

The way we transcend the limitations of the ego and these positionalities is that it gets such a tremendous payoff. This is where willingness really comes in. The willingness to be honest with yourself that the reason you cling to this is because of the payoff you're getting out of it. It's hard to admit that you love hating people. First of all, they deserve it. And hating them is a secret way of sort of getting even with them. You hit him with little hate thoughts out there, stab the person. You say, "I wouldn't think of that; that's like a witch would think that, no?" But that's what you're up to, aren't you? I see you—little stabbing thoughts.

Grief. People hang on to grief for lifetimes. About everything that's possible to die has died around you. How long are you going to hang on to the grief about that? I'll tell you how long to keep it: about one second. Let it go the instant you have it. Just let it go. Surrender it, completely and totally to God the *instant* it happens. Why? Because you develop the capacity to do that. So, the reason for spiritual training, then, is you develop a powerful capacity to let go of anything. And you never know when it's going to come up. "So and so" just died, just let it go that instant. The minute the phone message comes in, you let it go. You don't grieve about it 30 years later. You don't celebrate every anniversary of the death of Kuku, your little bird. Two weeks later, it's you've got to celebrate the death of Uncle Louis, and then a month later, it's time to celebrate the death of Aunt—then your mother's death comes up. The anniversary of all this shit. As you get older and older, the whole calendar is the anniversaries of crap.

We're going to keep pumping 9/11 forever. We've already got December 7. Then you've got 1776, you've got the end of World War I, and we've got November 11—don't forget November 11 at 11 A.M. When I grew up, it was November 11, at 11 A.M., Armistice Day. We all held our hearts. There's a beautiful value to it. I'm just telling you about the downside of it. It's one thing to give respect and send love to all those people, and to do so out of reverence. We're talking about the fact that what makes these things tenacious is, first of all, you're trained in them, your mind thinks this way, then after you are aware that you're trained in them and your mind thinks this way and you see the absurdity of the idea of causality, you'll find that your mind still wants to do this. And you say, "Why is my mind still doing that when I know better?" And a spiritual student usually goes into that, "I know better. How come I'm still hating that guy and want to get even with him? Why did I give him the finger?"

I told you the pleasure I got the first and only time I ever did it in my life. It was terrific! I can see why those guys are out there throwing stones at the Jews, and the Jews are throwing at the Arabs, and everybody is wanting to kill each other. I mean, it's terrific! Take that! *Whack, whack, whack, whack!* I mean, that's a high like—it beats riding bucking broncos, you know what I mean?

You see those guys out there at the rodeo. There was a whole bunch of them sitting behind me. They all have their own cast. They've all got all crippled up from riding these bulls, you know. Can't wait to get on the next one. The juice you get off of that, you know. I mean, this guy has got six fractures over the last five years riding bulls, and he's going to get right back on the next bull. Oh my gosh. Extreme sports, huh?

So Willingness, then, because that's one really important aspect of love. It's Willingness that's going to really take you up on the Map. Willingness is going to give you the motivation to accept things. It's also going to take you past Reason, which is the big roadblock. Most of the people who go into spiritual work are usually in the 400s; I mean many of them, who attend lectures like this, are usually in the 400s, in which Reason brings them here, and now, Reason becomes the block.

Because very few people get to Love. We said Love, to transcend the 400s, is accomplished by about 4 percent of the population, 4 percent. Whoa! To get to Unconditional Love is 0.4 percent; 0.4 percent. So, we talk about love a lot, but to realize one's identity as that which is the source of life itself is not all that easy to, I would not say "achieve," but that easy to realize. And therefore, I mention that the things that I think can be useful are generally available. Not everybody can go off and join an ashram. Not everybody can walk away from their family and their job, etc.

THE WILLINGNESS TO SURRENDER

So, how can this go, then? So, the willingness to let go of positionalities, the willingness to surrender, not the things themselves, but the attachment to the things themselves. You don't have to give up your Cadillac, um, but you let go of its former meaning to you. You let go striving for success because to realize the Truth is the epitome of success. To realize the truth of who you are.

So, renunciation, then, means eventually an inner renunciation. The willingness to let go of insisting that if a thing isn't logical, it can't be true, and all these kinds of positionalities. The willingness to then let go of everything that stands in the way of love. As we do that, we find that the things that keep coming up that block us from love, then, are feelings, and these feelings are based on certain perceptions, ways of seeing things, ways of interpreting them, conditionalities that we've been brainwashed into, and ask: "Am I willing to surrender that to God? Would I rather be right, or would I rather realize the Presence of God?" So, Willingness, then, always puts up the untruth against the Truth, and asks, "Are you are willing to let this go?"

To be unwilling to let go of attachment to kitty would mean grief, wouldn't it? You'd be setting yourself up for grief. If I lose the cat, tonight's going to be awful; tomorrow there won't be a lecture; I'm just going to be grieving, weeping, and gnashing my teeth, right? So, you see the unwillingness, then, is what sets you up for the lower levels on the Map. You say to yourself: "Am I willing to set myself up for this, or let it go?" Now, that makes it a little more real, doesn't it? If you're willing to let it go for some airy-fairy-sounding thing like the Presence of God, which sounds good, but who knows what that is. But you might be willing to let it go, because if you don't, this is where you're going to end up, low on the Map. Suffering from wantingness is endless suffering, isn't it, because wantingness, the constant wanting things is constantly setting you up with desire. You're always *wanting* something. I only have one want left in the world. I keep it there, cherish it. One worldly want.

I think, "God, can't I have just one?" I don't really have *it*; I have a picture of *it*. And I carefully nurture this want, because I'm afraid if it disappears, I'd become invisible. It keeps you here to some degree. You need one want and one attachment to *something*. I was showing people a picture of it yesterday. Anyway. The willingness to renounce it. Am I willing to renounce it? Yes. In fact, it just went.

So, what we're developing is the spiritual muscles so that when you need them, they're there. As I step over the rattlesnake, there I am at the top of Schnebly Hill. I was looking at a big place there, and as I step over it, good God Almighty, there is a hugest rattler you ever saw. Good Lord! And in that instant, there was letting go at *absolute* depth, an absolute letting go-ness. All fear disappeared, all perception of it as a possible enemy—and in its place there was a profound stillness and peace that was infinitely powerful. The presence of love, of the Presence of God is so powerful, it sweeps away everything. And so, the snake is held there, suspended—it's like that; it can't move. That profound state of peace, the stillness of the Presence of God, holds all within itself, and nothing can withstand it.

So, when you need it, that capacity was already perfected: to completely let go totally at great depth; otherwise, I wouldn't be here today, because the snake would have just done its snake

The Pathway of Love

thing, and I'd just do my human thing, and you know, we both would have been in trouble. So, a higher state prevailed. So, you never know when you're going to need this capacity. You have to be in—and one meditative style is to look at all the things in your life and keep surrendering what there is about it: aversion or attachment.

So, this is a willingness to surrender attachments and aversions. Do I really care if the rattlesnake kills me? To tell you the truth, no. Now, why not now? I mean, later it's certain. Why not now? What's the difference? You're going to leave the body any day, so whether it's today or tomorrow, it doesn't really make any difference, does it?

That capacity to surrender, then, to let go, is a form of love. See, we call Love a calibrated level of consciousness, but actually all these things from here up on the Map are all forms of Love. This is Love in the form of the capacity to tell the truth about yourself. That's why being sensitive is very indicative that you need help. If you get offended by things, feel uncomfortable about them, you'd better see your doctor, because if you really accept who you are, nothing can make you feel uncomfortable. Nothing can be injurious to your self-esteem, because if you're quite evolved, you don't have any self-esteem. How can people injure your self-esteem when you don't have any? I tell people: "What do you need self-esteem for?" Does a bird need self-esteem to fly? It doesn't need self-esteem. I mean, this is an appurtenance that you plaster around yourself. There's always somebody in the news at 6:30 whose sensitivities have been offended. You can't live in this world without offending somebody's sensitivities nowadays. You get up and give the lady your seat, and she feels offended because you're insulting her that the feminine is weaker than the male or something. You hold the door, or you don't hold the door, so I mean you're offending somebody, no matter what you do, you see what I mean? So, every night, somebody's offended by something. What was it this week? This week there was a group in Berkeley that might be offended if they showed the red, white, and blue on the campus. To celebrate 9/11, there's a group that politically felt people might be offended by showing the red, white, and blue on the campus. So, if you'd be offended by the flag, you'll be offended by anything. And lots of people are offended by God or any mention thereof. That's right, they have a political group, don't they? I forgot all about that. Remove God from everything—"*e pluribus something or other*"; "In Blank We Trust." The United States Treasury. The Constitution, we'll have to rewrite that; "Equality of man is guaranteed by the Divinity blank"; we'll have to delete Divinity of its origination.

When you totally accept the reality of who you are, you can't be offended. You're "Fatso"; they can call you any name they want to: "Shorty." "Four Eyes." "Dumbbell." Right! Somebody calls you a liar, you tell them, "I'm the best liar on the planet. You want to hire me? I'm worth a fortune." Yeah. You're bad-looking, I say, "Every time I look in the morning, I call 911. I look at myself in the mirror, and I call 911; I mean, I'm so ugly." You say, "The reason I have all these problems in life is because I'm so stupid and I'm so ugly." That's true. It's because I'm stupid.

You see, once you accept the possible downside of everything, nobody can offend you. "You're greedy." "Yeah, I *am* greedy. I'm Mister Greed, man. Give me what I want!" You know what I mean? You just become that which people say you are. You're impervious; there's nothing you can say. So, you see, we can't make neuroticism the law of the land. You're not going to be able to *not* offend somebody, see. Because some people are going to be offended if you *do*, and some people will be offended if you *don't*. Consequently, you're always going to offend somebody, so live with it. You're offended when you go through the line in the airport, so be offended; I mean, it's your problem if you're offended. That's the law of the land right now.

So, truth, then, what we call "truth," which is usually just "content," depends on "context." What's "truth" today is not "truth" tomorrow. What's appropriate today is not appropriate tomorrow. What's appropriate in "this" circumstance is not appropriate in "that" circumstance. The difficulty, then, with one's irrationality is, it doesn't understand that meaning comes out of context, not just content. So, the political position that's causing the most aggravation in society right now is the inability to discern that context totally changes content. What's suitable in peace is not the same as suitable in war. What's suitable in the inner city's streets is not suitable on Park Avenue inside itself. What is appropriate shifts depending on context. Who? When? The totality of the universe.

So, context is really the totality of the whole history of the entire universe. And, if people are going to insist on looking for a cause, we tell them the "cause" of it is the totality of the entire universe throughout all of time. And that's why this little piece of dust is sitting right where it is, you know. And, trying to pin it on me, man, forget it! It's the universe's fault. Ah, I'd be some lawyer, wouldn't I? I'd love to be a lawyer. I can see the lack of logic. And it's always one of confusing content—taking content out of context, and confusing the two, you see what I'm saying. And assuming causes when there is no such cause in the universe.

The willingness to let go all blocks, then. So, this is a form of love; this is the courage to accept the truth of who you are. "Yeah, I have a certain problem, and I'm going to go to a 12-step meeting about it." I told a lady that in the office this week. I thought she was going to buck me on it. She said, "Oh, I'm going to go to psych and back to meetings." Whoa, thank you, Lord! I don't have to argue with her. So, a lot of people hit bottom here. This is where you hit bottom. All this stuff here is taking you to the point that it's not working anymore, and suddenly you become quite open. Quite open.

And Neutral means "Yeah, I don't care if I go to the meetings or I do go to the meetings. If you say I should go to the meetings, then I'm willing, because I accept that I've got a problem and I understand that." And eventually out of lovingness—so the reason to continue it really is out of lovingness for yourself and others.

So this is the great block, though, level 200. This is the great block. Twenty-two percent of the population crosses this line. Eighty-seven percent is down below it. Eighty-seven percent can't use kinesiology to tell the truth about anything. It doesn't work for them.

The willingness to surrender all the blocks to love, then, are really what spiritual work is about. You don't have to seek love, you don't have to learn about love, there's nothing required about love, because when the blocks that prevent it are removed, it comes in like a tsunami; it just—*bam!*—wipes you out. And anybody who has been in that bliss state knows it's ultra-powerful. It just takes over and wipes out anything that is not love. What somebody did to you seems to be a reason to hate them—the willingness to let it go.

We are going to do a lecture on karma too, because these are all ways of undoing the blocks to enlightenment. The karmic propensity, then, you begin to suspect, is why you can't let go of this particular thing. After much prayer, after much psychotherapy, after much everything you can do, and you're still stuck there. Therefore, I think the next lecture is on karma in which we're going to use kinesiology to pick up what the block is. Now that you can see what it is, it's easy to let it go. But when you don't know what it is that's holding it there, you're sort of up against a block.

So, Love, then, is a style, a way of being, and it's a way of being with yourself. Out of compassion for yourself, you're willing to let go of the things that bring you pain. So, instead of going from the bottom up, we can just start from the top down on the Map. Out of compassion for yourself, then, you're willing to let go of that which brings you pain, suffering, guilt—brings it to yourself and others. Out of love for yourself, out of love for oneself, out of compassion for oneself. Out of compassion for myself, I am not going to allow myself to fall into the pit. Not being so linked to something, that if it leaves, I will then go into grief. Out of compassion. So, that lovingness now takes the form of an attitude toward yourself and your own life and those around you. So out of compassion for everything, then, I have the willingness to let things go.

We do it all the time as a style of life. One expression of love, then, is devotion, and in spiritual work, that devotion becomes more and more intense. It finally reaches the point where it's willing to let *anything* go that stands in the way. We may think it's the small things that we're letting go of. We say, "Well, I let go of my favorite sneakers and it seems trivial." Oh no. The capacity to let go of your favorite sneakers and not grieve about them or be angry at somebody stealing them or something. The capacity to surrender your sneakers is going to be one of the last things right before enlightenment. Why is that? It's because you have that capacity to let go, huh? You try and get some people to let go of something; it's really something. You just cannot pry them loose, you know. "You're gonna go to jail if you don't do it; everybody's going to leave you; you're going to die of it." I mean, they won't let go. It's like they are in a spasm, you know.

The capacity to learn to let things go, you learn to do it with small things. Could you let go of being mad at that guy for cutting in front of you in traffic? That's a wonderful example. Every day you get all these spiritual opportunities. Say, "Go ahead, man, it's all right. Go ahead—SOB." After a while, you let go of the SOB and you say, "Oh well, we'll get there at the same time anyway." You know, rationality, "I'm only going to get there three seconds later, big deal." So, then you are trying it with logic, see? You're trying to think, "So, I've let go of all this stuff at the bottom and decided not to kill him. And he's not really causing me any problem with pride because he's a better driver than I am."

You're all the way up to Reason. Reason says, "Eh, a couple of seconds this way, a couple of seconds that way. It's all the same, you know what I mean?" But we're getting there, so we're developing the tools and the techniques. The most powerful thing you'll need is really powerful capacities in the one-pointedness of mind to go the whole way in Nonduality and Zen and advanced Buddhism. This is a capacity that you learn. And then, when you really need it, because you're going to run into tests that are really quite powerful—stronger than what you think, both over it and not so over it. Because, as you move ahead, that which is made uncomfortable or displaced in its control over and influence over mankind, begins to get annoyed that you're moving out of that

KARMA AND DEVOTION

domain and threatening their domain. And so, you start getting the challenges.

When the challenges come up, that's when you need the tools. So, spiritual work then, out of love and compassion for yourself, and out of love for God, devotion to God, you develop these strengths, these capacities, this discernment. And, eventually, it's like a knife, you can cut through anything. You can lose anything and everything, disconnect: parents, grandparents, country, lovers, wives, children, dogs, cats, houses, titles, anything! *Whoosh!* In an instant, it's gone. So, that laser-like one-pointedness of mind and the willingness to cut through anything, no matter what it is, is what's going to be needed at a later date. So, we perfect it every day. We perfect that capacity. So, that's a form of Love. All of spiritual work is a form of Love. We surrender it all as a form of devotion. "Out of my love for Thee, O Lord, I let go my attachment to so-and-so. I surrender it to Thee." The willingness to let go of anything and everything to God. In the end, you're asked to let go all of it, even physicality. Yeah, even physicality.

And of course, the ultimate one, which we will talk about at the end of the lectures, is the willingness to give up what you think is the source of life itself. You're asked to give up life for God. And you see that the ego is coming to its end, but you don't know it's just the ego; you think it's *you*. And your willingness to surrender life itself as you understand it, to God, is going to require all the strength that you've learned. So, devotion, then, is a one-pointed, um, willingness, and it becomes tested all the time. The expression of love as devotion, then, becomes the core of many forms of devotion, whether Christianity or Zen meditation. . . .

So, in strict meditation, then, it's really one's devotion that carries you through the practice. It can keep you sitting there for eight hours nonstop, no problem. It can keep you sitting there 12 hours nonstop. It can keep you sitting there until you don't know what happened, but you apparently fell over from dehydration or something. It could be a couple of days later, and you have no memory of it. That capacity, then, becomes perfected, and it is a way of devotion to your own spiritual evolution. One becomes

The Pathway of Love

devoted to the evolution, and you see that this is a commitment to God and to all the higher beings that are calling you to do so.

People say, "How do I know I'm going to be enlightened someday or something?" Well, I tell them, "If you weren't destined to be enlightened, you wouldn't be in this lecture." Nobody who's not destined to be enlightened would even be here. Who would be at a class on how to drive a speedboat? Only people who are going to get a speedboat; I mean, nobody else is going to be there. By definition, the people who are interested in enlightenment are the people who are going to become enlightened. I mean, that's how you get there, isn't it? Unless you're one of those drop-off-the-cliff enlightenments. They happen too.

Just as you go over the side, you completely and totally surrender everything to God. You go into an incredible state. Much to your dismay, you wake up four days later in a hospital. Everybody's saying, "Oh, it's so wonderful you're still alive!" You're going, "Man, I was in heaven and they resuscitated me . . . thanks a lot!" "Yeah, they took me right out of that bliss, I'm really happy about that." Any of you who have had near-death experiences know the humor of that one.

HUMOR AS AN EXPRESSION OF LOVE

So, it's possible to stay in a very good state all the time, and one of the expressions of Love is humor. Why? Because humor recontextualizes all of life in such a way that you can handle it without resorting to any of the lower levels. There's nothing to be angry about if you see that it's sort of absurd, you know what I mean? I won't even say it. Anyway. It's a way of staying in the world.

To recontextualize things. What is it? It's comparing the context of Reality with the content of appearance, and you see the absurdity of the comparison, I guess. So, that humor is one style. And people who become spiritually evolved often become quite comical because they wear the world lightly, you know, like a garment, and everything sort of becomes comical.

And, um, you know, because of the contrast with Reality, the absurdity. So, it's the absurdity, it's the theater of the absurd that is comical. People don't expect that. They expect piety. Well, piety *is* profound. And the difficulty I had this morning was that I didn't know if I was going to function because, in a state of bliss, you see, as you let go of all these things, progressively life becomes more beautiful and more harmonious. The miraculous takes care of everything. A sense of inner joy begins to arise. It becomes so severe that it can be ecstatic. In a state of Ecstasy, you really cannot function in the world. In the state of high Joy, you can't really function in the world. And in the state of bliss, um, you just sit there. I thought, "Maybe I'll just bless everybody today." But I managed to get out of it with the help of people. Because this morning, I thought, "Oh, wow." I mean, yeah. The state, you know.

So, having been with it for some years, one learns how to sort of be with it, more or less; but then, at times it becomes quite profound—it cannot be denied, and it just wipes you out. That's why it's good to have friends that know what you are about, friends that understand it. Be associated with spiritual groups. You know, I was a psychiatrist for some years, many years for the Episcopal diocese, the Catholic diocese, the Catholic nuns, the Zen monastery, the ministry, for many years and, uh, I had to discern the difference between these states. Is this guy in a state of *samadhi*, or is he catatonic? He came down from the Zen monastery. Borderline schizophrenia is not a good condition with which to start a Zen meditation, because pretty soon things start talking to you and flying around. Is this a state of Ecstasy, true Spiritual Ecstasy, or is it religious mania? Hard to differentiate. I can think of moments in my life if a psychiatrist was examining me, he would probably have ordered Thorazine. So, that was really my function: Does he need Thorazine, or should we all bow to him, you know what I'm saying? Because those high states can be very, very powerful. Ecstasy and Joy and the one that takes us out of the world, the one that took us out this morning, was bliss. *Satchitananda*. The presence becomes so profound that one really becomes immobilized by it.

The Pathway of Love

See, the purposes of a church, the beauty, the sanctity, the music, and the mantras, the pageantry, the stained-glass windows, the incense. When you try to figure out how to work your computer in that state, huh? What computer?

Ah, that's 740, and it makes you weep and immobilizes you in a state of exquisite beauty. Exquisite beauty of the Presence of God. And so, you can see why you need friends, because when you go into that state profoundly, you really can't function. And, so, we'll take a break now that we can't function. If you allow that state to continue, you have to stop lecturing. You can see it immobilizes you.

[Q]: "Isn't everyone who is not in this room also destined for enlightenment?"

"No!" Miss these lectures and you've had it, you know what I'm saying! No, it's an interesting question because it brings up other dimensions ruled by entities who hate God, refuse God, and consciously refuse God. The lower astral regions are those who hate God, refuse God, when given the opportunity to choose God, have said no. And they perpetuate for eons, and that's who rules the lower astral domains, is those who've refused God and deny God, and therefore they are not destined for enlightenment.

So, one of the forms of Love that we didn't get a chance to talk about this morning is the classic yoga, called "karma yoga." You know, the great yogas through the heart, through nonduality, through mind. The third great one, which characterizes Christianity and characterizes, in fact, all spiritually motivated people is karma yoga, the yoga of service. Krishna speaks of that. It brings up something extremely important: that what spiritual work is really about is a recontextualization of your whole life and everything in it. So, devotion, the Pathway of Love, is sanctifying all of your life in all of its details and all its expressions as an expression of love to God and to all that exists.

So, as you take that little ring off the top of your stove, that goes around the burner there, and you take the steel wool and you really polish it so it shines; you do so because everything that exists, exists because innately, it's divine. Once you see the Divinity of all things—watering the garden, shining your shoes—all are equal. All are done as. . . . So, as a devoted being, all your actions become those of devotion of service to others, service to God. Service to others is service to God. Without the dozen or so people it took to set up this conference, who all did it out of devotion into all hours of the night—"Aren't you ever going to go to bed?" So, their devotion is behind their work: the endless phone calls, the endless faxes, the endless letters; answering all that's required to just put it together is a rather staggering amount of work. So, their devotion.

So, the commitment, then, to God is a devotional statement: "That I am what I am, and all that I do is for Thy sake, O Lord." Not that God needs it. People think worship and all that sacrifice is giving something to God. Guilt, penance, wearing ash cloth and ashes, and crawling on your knees until they bleed, across the cobblestones, which we have all done in some lifetime, doesn't turn God on: "Man, I get off on suffering, you know what I mean?" What is he, weird? No, it's because in our own belief system then, our understanding of God—or misunderstanding of God—is that we do this out of devotion to God. So, you know, to become a true spiritual seeker, you really are sanctifying your whole life and everything in it, to God, and to the service of Truth and that which makes the Presence of God more apparent to others.

When you sanctify all that you do, then, you take it from the mundane into a different realm because you're putting it in a different context. And power comes out of context. It's the context that gives all that exists its power. It's out of context that you survive from moment to moment. Once you see that that which you are is always existence, its survival was never threatened in the first place. And all the worries you ever had were ridiculous.

If, karmically, when you leave this world is already set—which it is—then, obviously you had to get there. In order to die at a prescribed point in time, you must have survived long enough to get there, so you can quit worrying about survival, because between now and the time you die, your survival is guaranteed. Between

The Pathway of Love

now and the time you die, your survival is guaranteed, so stop worrying about it. Whether you go from "this" or go from "that" is irrelevant, isn't it? Whether you go over a cliff or from whatever, it doesn't really make any difference.

We've said that before—that the time of your death is already karmically destined from the moment of your birth. To know that when you leave here is already preset, you can quit worrying about it, you know? People want you to do this, you'll live longer; do that, you'll live longer. I mean, it's absurd. How are you going to get out of this world, folks? I mean, they close all the doors—you can't die of this, you can't die of that—I mean, what's going to happen? You're going to become immortal? Can you imagine what you're going to look like when you're 150? I mean, like all these guys killing themselves for God, and then they're going to get 70 virgins when they get there. I always joke, "Yeah, but they're 900 years old." Heaven is not really a bordello, you know.

So, humor about it is better than being angry, being vicious, you know, because humor is a form of compassion. You understand that people who are innocent are easily misled; they're easily taken over by that which is ungodly, and the most common way to take over is to claim the name of God and then be up to something horrible but do it in the name of God. So, anyway, that for which usurps the name of God has its own karma to account. And that was why the first question we got was no. People who do that are not destined for enlightenment. To rape the innocent, the spiritually innocent with that which is fallacious and leads in the opposite direction, must have a karma too horrible to think about. I don't even want to think about it.

Then, we get very specific questions. Spirituality, then, to be a seeker, to be a devotee, or whatever you want to call it, to be a monk, to be a layman, to walk about in a contemplative state no matter what you do, that's because you've contextualized your life in a different manner. Once you've sanctified your own life, and: "I surrender my life to Thee, O Lord."

You can talk about love, but when it takes over, you can't talk anymore. The surrender to God at great depth is overwhelming.

And that was what brought on the state that occurred in 1965. And swept away everything, for many years.

* * *

The Urantia Book: we get asked a lot of details about specific gurus, specific books. We're working now—we just finished *I*. And then, after we finish that, we're already halfway through another book in which we do about a thousand calibrations because, first of all, not everybody's got the time to do them; you've got to go to work, you've got family and kids, you can't just stand around, gathering stuff all day. And people don't have faith in their own capacity; they want confirmation. So, we're doing about a thousand calibrations of things that we think would be of interest. It's like you're going from black and white into technicolor. When you add calibrations to everything that ever occurred, from the great pyramids, to all the great cathedrals, all the great composers, to all the great philosophers, scientists, works of art, music, not only throughout history but contemporary, you get a totally different understanding of life and its expressions. Totally different understanding. Much greater depth. You finally go, "Oh, I see. Oh, I see. Oh, I see." So, you go through an aha experience.

First time I was a teacher of *A Course in Miracles*, I had a secretary back east, and we were comparing . . . she was making a list of ego positions and their spiritual corollary, and as she was typing it up, she went into a bliss state. She wasn't even interested in the subject, she said. God bless her heart. She was my secretary back east for some 20 years. Anyway, she just blissed out, just from the material. So, I feel it would be greatly valuable, and we're trying to find out how to write it without hurting anybody's feelings, but I don't know if that's going to be possible. We could just stick to dead people, but they've got descendants. You know, my great-great-great grandfather was. . . . So, anyway, how to express that:

There are so many books. We've advised you to go through your spiritual library, see what makes you go strong, see what makes you go weak. Those that make you go weak, throw them away, but leave them in a pile and don't throw them out right away.

Leave them there for a week. Because you walk by them every day, you finally "get it." "Wow, I see what the difference is," you know? All the end-times books and all that kind of stuff is all over here, you see. Those things which are eternal Truths—you can tell that which is True has been agreed upon by every enlightened being throughout all of time. There is absolutely no disagreement about anything, between all enlightened beings. It's always been exactly the same. Anything that varies from that is not the truth.

And we make that rather specific in the book we just finished, but I thought the next book, where we calibrate about a thousand things, tells you where it all is. Now, everything doesn't have to be 1000 to be useful, you know what I'm saying? If you're down here, something that calibrates at 180 is going to be very good, you know what I'm saying? If you're in Apathy, if you can get up to wanting something, you've made a big move out of the wastebasket, crawling across on your bare knees, beating yourself, falling over, crying all the time, quivering, laying there paralyzed with fear. If you can get pissed about something, you're going to at least move your body in some kind of positive direction, because you know how to win and get out of this freaking state you're in. Don't forget, whole continents live here. Whole continents are born in this level down here. Whole continents, whole countries. We live in a civilized society that calibrates around 430, and we think that's what's normal. That's what is normal for us, but it's definitely not what's normal for other people.

The different countries of the world and continents and what is the calibrated levels—the energies of those various societies, those various countries—it gives you quite an understanding of politics. Without those calibrations, you don't really understand politics, because you're coming at it from your position, you know. Your position is not what prevails elsewhere in this world at all, not at all. I've been in places in a country where a whole family of 20 lives in a couple of cardboard boxes put together with string, and they take turns sleeping in it and digging up roots. They do not live in your world at all.

So, I thought about the different countries and continents and about where they're at. It gives you an understanding of why we seem to be. . . . if you're a political diplomat, you really have to understand these things. The terrible mistakes we make militarily and diplomatically and politically is a total failure to comprehend where these other people are at. They're not anywhere at where what you are talking about. That's the trouble with academic views of things, politically correct things, because you live in an airy-fairy world. You know, people don't live there. People also have bodies. They forget that.

Anyway, The Urantia Book. Let's see, do we have permission to do that? I'm familiar with The Urantia Book, from many years ago. "Urantia, we have permission?" [True.] "It's over 200-resist." [True.] "Thank God. It's over 300." [True.] "350?" [Not true.] So it's in the high 300s. So, you see, each of these teaching methods is appropriate for certain levels. We said there are not really "higher" or "lower" levels because you're learning tools, and these tools are useful when you're at 800, just like they're useful when you're at 200. So, if your own calibrations are down below 200, let's say your life is horrible and you decide to quit drinking and you go to AA, you take the first step. That takes you over 200 right there.

You say, 200 won't take you all the way to enlightenment. Oh, yeah, it will because without courage, you're not going to take any of these other steps. Each one of these is a brick, is a brick. So, none of them is really *higher* than the other. This is the way the calibrated scale came out, and I had, uh, it just came out, you know, by questioning. This is the way it came out.

These things are very, very necessary. Without the capacity to face the Truth about yourself, you're not going to move up any higher. So, here we have something that calibrates in the 300s, and so to move out of here, all this stuff up here is meaningless. I read this very erudite book last night. I just skimmed through it in a hurry to see what I could get out of quantum mechanics and its application to consciousness, and there wasn't anything of any use in there. It calibrated around 450; well, I know all that. That's just, you know, intellectualism and logic and computers and mathematics. The mathematics of consciousness is one thing, but consciousness is something totally different, to which you cannot apply mathematics, actually. But I'm looking for that interface between the linear and the nonlinear, which was the point of writing *Power vs. Force*. And again, in the conclusion of *I*, I have a little appendix at the end on quantum mechanics because the quantum potentiality is that space where, from the viewpoint of common logic, you can see that that to which logic is not applicable, can also exist, because that which is hardcore scientism denies anything other than the linear reality could exist. And I want to show that *au contraire*. *Au contraire*. The very reason you say that is because of that which is nonlinear, which is dominating your consciousness, and which you are not going to find out with mathematics. You only find it out through meditation.

MUSCLE TESTING AND INTEGRITY

The method of kinesiology . . . as I've said, we're not kinesiologists. It's only a technique that we use for the sake of spiritual research and for comprehending the nature of life and illuminating things for which there is no other tool possible. And we do somewhat review it each time, each lecture, that two people have to be over 200. The purpose of the question has to be integrous; you make it in the form of a statement, and before you do it, you have to ask if you have permission to do it. You say, "I have permission to do this," and then the person resists. And, not infrequently, you get a no. If you're curious and you've got time, you can research the reason for the no. A lot of times we're in a hurry, and we just want a yes or no for, let's say, "Should we turn left or right?" I don't need to know the reason.

And sometimes couples are not good with each other. I don't know why, marital couples. We just haven't had time to research why that is. Sometimes a couple will have to find a third party, and with them, they're fine. There's methods of doing it by yourself.

So, everybody knows this method here, the so-called thumb and middle finger, which you hold as tight as you can. Now, you picture Jesus Christ. You try to break it; you see with this if you can break it. Now, I'm going to hold in mind somebody who has been on TV a lot lately.

Anyway, so that's a technique you can use by yourself. And then we found that 10 percent of the general population can't do it. "Ten percent of people who are entitled to do it are unable to do it-resist." [True.] Huh! "And that's due to some strangeness about their chi energy-resist." [True.] "And that chi energy has to do with karma." [True.] It has something to do with karma. So, karmically, some people have some problem with their chi energy, that about 10 percent of those who are entitled to kinesiology are unable to do it, so within those limitations.

The other thing about spirituality is that you want to know specific things about things that are very applicable in a very wide variety of expressions. And sometimes people use it to ask questions that are really sort of irrelevant, you know what I mean? Yeah. We *were* going to use it to find kitty yesterday, but kitty showed up. I asked the Holy Spirit to find kitty, and sure enough, Lou hopped up and there was kitty. He found kitty. Susan realized where it was. She said, "Oh, I know where it is, behind so-and-so's house." Lou went over there, and sure enough, there it was. And then, we also got a present of a bunch of books on kitties; so somehow, kitty-ness, you know, that energy field coalesced, discovered kitty, and at the same time, somebody said, "Here's a present for you." I opened it and it was four little books on kitties. It's just sort of funny. So, that's the one you can use for yourself.

Now, the question about President Bush comes up. I do a lot of radio programs, and we're going to do one in November in Scottsdale. Let's see, we've got one in October, we're going to do at Church of Agape, which is in L.A. In November, we're going to do one in Scottsdale, with Mishka Productions, which is associated with Hay House. I do a number of radio programs, and a lot of them are fun. These interviewers are fun people, and they have a comical way of expressing things. A week or two ago, we did a radio and a TV one right after that. Anyway, we had a good time with it. But this question about President Bush comes up all the time, and you

The Pathway of Love

can tell the political slant of the radio interviewer or whoever it is, you know. He's sort of like, "Tell us why President Bush is wrong." You shouldn't ask a question with kinesiology unless you're prepared for the answer. Sometimes I get letters from people: "What do you think about guru Baba so-and-so?" Well, I know from just looking at him and picking up his energy, he's about 140. So, am I going to answer this, and upset this person, who's going to lie awake and think he's given everything away for Baba so-and-so, and the guy calibrates at 140? Or what should I do?

As far as President Bush, let's say, we said the office of the presidency runs around 450. Roosevelt was like 499. To run a government, you should really be in about the mid-400s. If you get too high—Einstein's 499—and Einstein wouldn't be too good at running a government, you know. So, you need to be around 450. That's where Bush is, around 450, 460; that is capable, that's logic, that's reason. It's sane; it is geared to this world. It's not off in "la-la land," nor is it into the spleen or even personal ambition, which would be the solar plexus. No, it's integrous. Don't forget: That which is over 200 is integrous. So, that is where we would want the presidents to be. If he gets too much up high on the Map, he's not going to be useful anymore. He'd be like the pope. Mother Teresa—you can't have Mother Teresa running a government, you know what I'm saying. You've got to be with this world and its political realities, so to be appropriate, you have to be appropriate to where you are. So, that's why one number is not *better* than another number.

I remember going into a boxing ring one time in 1945, or whenever it was. I went aboard this ship, a minesweeper, hazardous duty in the South Pacific. And a young guy, who's still a friend of mine, Jimmy Sanders, ah, anyway, there was only 18 of us in this crew, you know. Anyway, I come ashore, and these guys there have got tattoos, earrings, and stuff. I mean, they were grizzly-looking guys who'd been out to sea for a while. So, this guy says, "Hey, Shorty." That was my name henceforth—"Shorty" or "Four Eyes." Anyway, I took my glasses off. "Shorty," he says, "You know how to box?" I said, "Well, I had lessons with Richie Mitchell, who was the former middle-weight champion of the world in Milwaukee."[1] As a kid, I was always getting beat up. So, my grandfather took me to Richie Mitchell's gym and said, "Teach him how to fight." I was never interested in fighting, and all these gruesome wrestling crap that kids did. I mean, lots of kids were disgusting when I was a kid. Always picking their nose and wanting to stick their gooey fingers in your eye and wrestle you; I mean they were sweaty, and oh my god, anyway, these horrible kids. So, he says, "You got to teach him how to box." So, I went to Richie Mitchell, and I was a mosquito weight. Fly weight was the smallest they had. Anyway, I was a mosquito weight.

So, I learned how to box, and after I learned how to box . . . you know, we had choir practice two nights a week. I was in the choir. I was an acolyte, and when the bishop walked around, I went by his side and held his robes and did the incense and all, and I sang "Panis Angelicus" as a boy soprano in the great cathedral with incense and stained glass, and I tell you, if that doesn't bring on the tears to your eyes, wow, it knocked me out.

So, I was a mosquito weight, and the way I won after that. . . . The first fight after that, I won. I was so fast that he didn't know what hit him, and I always hit him in the nose—*wham*, like that!—and then I was out before he could hit me. He'd get a bloody nose, end of fight. So, I go in the navy, and Jimmy Sanders says to me: "Hey, Shorty." That was my name thereafter; you can't be too sensitive about things. And he says, "You know how to box?" I said, "Yeah. I took lessons with Richie Mitchell." "Wow," he said. "We'll go up in the gun tub and go a round." So, we go up like this, and one shot and I was unconscious. He hit me once. Later I found out that he was champion of the Third Fleet. He was the most fiercesome boxer I've ever seen. He was ferocious and fast. God bless him.

So after not hearing from these people for 50 years, my mates on the ship—after 50 years, after the war is over—all of a sudden, I start hearing from them. Imagine that—50 years, and suddenly

---

1 Although he was technically a lightweight and lost the championship to Benny Leonard, Richie Mitchell was still a legendary fighter.

The Pathway of Love

some guy calls me and says, "Are you Dave Hawkins?" "Yeah." "Are you Shorty?" I said, "Yeah. I'm still short, yeah." He told me who he was, and we both broke into tears. So, everybody that . . . then we found each other, and as each one would call, we would always break into tears. I would break into tears; the guy at the other end would break into tears. You see, because that love, that love there was beyond all time. So, one characteristic of love, you see, is that which your mates back in World War II—there was a love there that was incredible, and it lasted forever. Lasted forever. Fifty years, you didn't hear from them and it was like yesterday. You break into tears. So that commitment to love, then, is beyond time, beyond assailing. I don't care what he's done in the meantime. It's all irrelevant. It's only the reality of the reconnection with love as a state of mind.

What occasioned the jump over the 200s? Well, we said the most incredible thing that ever happened, I think, other than the great gurus, the great Avatars, was in the late '80s when consciousness level went from 190 to 207. As I've said before, it was at the time of the Harmonic Convergence; it was at the time of World Peace Day; everybody woke up at four o'clock, and we all prayed for peace. All those things occurred at the same time. And at about the same time, monolithic communism fell over, and many other events. But, the destiny of mankind, then, has become quite different. The destiny of man at 207 is considerably different than 190; 190 means endless hell. And 207 means only localized hell. It means sort of that mankind is going to progress.

I'm just telling you things that are in the book I'm finishing now, but we'll ask about it. "In the book, we announce that evolution of mankind is progressing, and partly his nervous system is changing-resist." [True.] "In order to be able to handle higher energies-resist." [True.] "Mankind up to now could only handle an energy up to 1000-resist." [True.] "Now, very rarely, but on occasion, it can go over a 1000-resist. [True.] "That's the first time in history-resist." [True.] "It presages the evolution, the appearance of a new *Homo spiritus*-resist." [True.] The evolution of *Homo spiritus*. You see, *Homo sapiens* came off there. But to handle higher

KARMA AND DEVOTION

energies, you really need a different nervous system; this nervous system is horrendous if you're going to go over 600. It's not made to go over 600. You really need a different nervous system.

So, in a way, it presaged, to me, the prophesied return of Christ to earth. To me, the return of Christ to earth is not a physicality. It's the return of consciousness that will dominate mankind, because up until the late '80s, mankind was dominated by energies that were satanic and Luciferic, primarily.

Mankind was only interested in killing each other. The great hordes that came down on Europe and the Roman Empire—the only thing they were interested in was slaughtering everybody. They slaughtered them all, killed them. And then they made the great discovery that live people were worth more than dead people. And slavery was born. You see, if we recontextualize slavery, it was a great advance. Instead of getting slaughtered by the tens of thousands, we now corralled 5,000 and we sold you off. And, of course, the buyer was buying you like cattle, and cattle are worth money, so they saw to it that you were fed and basically taken care of. The alternate was just to be killed on the battlefield and die of your wounds. So, rather than dying slowly of your wounds on the battlefield, you got to work for somebody else. And, I think, in a certain way, you earned a certain karma by doing so. The willingness to surrender one's life to service.

That service may take all different kinds of forms, depending on what your level of consciousness is. So, service means something different at a lower level. Service out of love to God will mean something quite different here than it will from here, above 200. There, service to God might mean, to you, the willingness to kill Americans for God. That's how it's being held in mind, truly, by the field. I think the naive are brainwashed that way. I think that those who brainwash them are not deluded and don't really believe that at all, but they know it works. Let's see if that's so. "Those who blow themselves up to kill Americans for Allah are intrinsically naive-resist." [True.] "Intrinsically have been spiritually raped-resist." [True.] "Intrinsically have been brainwashed-resist." [True.] "The source of their brainwasher is, um, not

The Pathway of Love

innocent-resist." [True.] "He is *aware* of what it's doing." [True.] "It comes from the lower astral-resist." [True.] So, those are the people who are destined not to be enlightened. To rape the innocence of the spiritually pure and tell them to do that which is the opposite.

Now, actually, to a certain degree, you can. Because, you see, your consciousness, a great deal of it can be looking in one direction and part of it looking at another. You know you can be walking through the park, and also looking for a gumball machine. In other words, you're not losing contact with the whole park just because you're looking at a gumball machine. And yet if you don't parcel out part of your attention. . . . So, part of your attention is focused here. In spiritual work, it's quite a subtle balance between how much energy is "within" and how much is "without," how much is into context and how much is into content.

The prevailing technique that I suggest to people is one really of contemplation. It's really a contemplation in a way, an ongoing thing of its own. That, as things arise, one spontaneously, after a while, becomes spontaneous, surrenders them to God, and relinquishes one's attachment. As the fear that kitty is lost arises, the fear is instantly—the spiritual master within me *demands* now that I release it as it arises. Within one minute later, it's no longer there.

So, we surrender things to God as they arise, in the very process of arrivingness. So, surrendering is a continuous process. The fixity of focus; I could say I've been in fixity of focus when in the world, at least it was, the surrenderingness of everything as it arises. Whether 10 million die in a civil war in a certain place in the world is irrelevant. It's irrelevant whether 10 million die. But you have to be in a certain space to understand the truth of that. First of all, no death is possible. The quality of life is such that it is not possible for life to die. It's a good thing in spiritual work to get over the fear of death. One needs to realize that it is set already, and you don't experience it anyway. Nobody can experience their own physical death. We reaffirm that each time. "It's not possible to experience your own physical death-resist." [True.] Correct. You cannot experience your own death. First of all, it's set; secondly, you're not going to experience it anyway. Thirdly, life is not capable of being killed. The intrinsic essence and quality of life is that it is indestructible. "That's a fact." [True.] It's like the law of the conservation of matter. The law of conservation of life is even more true. Life can change form, but you cannot kill life. It's not possible to kill life.

The minute you swat a fly, he goes right off into his etheric body, and he keeps right on flying, and then he gets reborn as another fly. Hardly notices the difference. "Wasn't I here before?" he says to himself. "I don't remember if I was on this ship or not, was I? This is where the hamburgers are, oh yeah."

Because life cannot be destroyed, there is no point in mourning death. No death is possible. So, what are you crying about? What are you fearing? What are you saying? Isn't it awful 30 million died? Why is it awful? It's awful to you? Somebody tells you that's bad? Common belief is that it's bad. So, you keep surrendering things until one has completely and totally surrendered all of life to God. Everything as it arises. And then you realize that what you have been surrendering wasn't a reality in the first place. All the great sacrifices you thought you were making were all illusions. Sacrificing your physicality to God. You thought you were surrendering your life to God. You weren't surrendering your life to God. Life cannot be surrendered to anything. Life is ongoing, forever. Because life itself *is* the expression of God. Unless you can kill God, you can't kill life. We have our preferences. So, all you're letting go is preferences. A preference to continue as this physicality and its story, and you become enamored of its story. It isn't that you aren't willing to die; it's just that you don't want to give up the story.

What's more fascinating than the story of your own life? Tell me—nothing. I mean, it's entrancing, isn't it? It's the great romance of all time. Because we're all in love with ourselves secretly. And our story *is* the greatest story. And, uh, well, anyway.

The Pathway of Love

[Q]: *"When dying, does going into the light keep you in the cycle of reincarnation?"*

Well, it's asking about reincarnation, which is really next month's lecture. Jumping the gun. It has to do with the sense of the reality of that which is experiencing what it is experiencing. The only death that's possible is death of the ego. There's only one death possible—one only has to die once in all these lifetimes. You can live 10,000 lifetimes, but you're only going to die once, and that's one of the requirements to reach enlightenment. And the requirement is the willingness to die. Because you don't get any chance to die. You get hit by a bolt of lightning, and—zip—you just go out. It's great, being out. There's the body all fried up there: "Well, that was a killer, that one!" You're allowed so many deaths, you know; they pile up over time. Dying at the oars. That was a victory. So, each death seems to accomplish some great gain, you know. When I died at the oars, I surrendered and I thought, "They can't keep me tied to this goddamn thing." And I just let myself die, and instantly I was out of it. "Whoa, I'm free as a bird!"

So, each death, then, seems to have within it a spiritual lesson. The only *one* death you can actually do, which we won't really get up to until the last lecture, there's only one death you actually experience. And that *is* the experience of death itself. It's the only time you've ever had a chance to experience it, and it's the only time you'll ever have to go through it. And people need to be coached in advance about that state, because if you're a serious spiritual student, sooner or later, you'll meet that door. So, that'll be the last lecture—how to get through that door. There's only one death hereafter.

So, the preparation for what's required at the final door is what is going on now. Your devotion to God has to be *absolute*. The devotion to God has to supersede all else. And that's what carries you through the final door, is the willingness to surrender what *you* think and believe in your most inner conviction is life itself.

We said, "Attractor fields." We said from the viewpoint of nonlinear dynamics, chaos theory, each of these fields that calibrates here, is a calibrated field of energy at the center of which there is a so-called "attractor field." There's an "attractor field." You might picture it like when you see the birds as they swing about in a huge flock in the design that they play. What you're seeing is the demonstration of an inner, invisible attractor field. That attractor field is dominating them. So, what you think is that each bird is following another bird, like pilots in the sky. No, they're not. Each bird is following his own inner song; his own inner song is telling him to go this way. And this bird's inner song is also telling him to go this way, and this bird's inner song. Each bird is independently controlled by the energy field. They are not controlled by each other. They're not like pilots, 10 feet from you, 10 feet from you, 32 feet from you, 44 feet from you, and so on. That's the ego's view of it. No. Each of these birds is surrendered to be the servant of its inner guide, and it goes as it's guided by the inner attractor field. And the way we isolate and identify an attractor field is really by kinesiology.

The number of people over 200, we say it's increased, yes. When we wrote the book in '95, I think we did the calibrations in '94. Consciousness level we said that . . . I forget all these numbers now, but the number of people on the planet who have risen in their level of consciousness has increased quite a bit. It was 80 percent of the people were less than 200; now it's only 78 percent. So, the consciousness level of mankind is constantly rising. I mean, groups like this in the spiritual work they do, you know, affects the whole field of consciousness. The ripples that go out are affecting the whole field of consciousness.

So, all the people in the world committed to the evolution of consciousness radiate out into the field, and that field is like the sea, and that sea then supports the consciousness of everyone. People elsewhere wake up in the morning, and they suddenly make a different decision today than they have made all their life. "I've always thought this way," and suddenly they say, "You know, I could see it *this* way." Well, that energy out there makes it harder to be negative. So, it's harder to be negative now than it was. It's very hard to be negative. I mean, you gotta work at it nowadays,

The Pathway of Love

you know. You've got to go off on some god-awful place on the planet, listen to some really weird people, and get brainwashed in order to be that way, you know; now it's hard to do that.

[Q]:"Do the demands of ordinary life interfere with spiritual evolution and work?"

No. As we said, everything gets contextualized differently now. Everything gets contextualized. And you shine everything out of love for God. You sweep the floor out of devotion to one's children and family. You peel the potatoes for the same reason.

[Q]: "Can techniques which lower one's brain wave frequency also raise one's level of consciousness?"

Hmm, I don't know, I never asked that. "What they're meaning here is, uh . . . what they are talking about here is alpha wave training-resist." [True.] "The answer to this is yes." [True.] Huh, says yes. There are various techniques.

The more advanced your consciousness gets, the slower your brain waves get. And finally, they become ridiculously low. You wonder how you survive. Anyway, there is a brain wave every once in a while that keeps you going. To function effectively in the world, you've got to have 15 cycles per second, 14 or 15. So, I have great hopes that President Bush is running at about 400; he's running at beta rhythm, 10 to 14, whatever it is.

THE SPIRITUAL WARRIOR

We didn't really answer the Bush question. The Bush question is one in which how you contextualize it. To defend one's honor, to defend the innocent, to stand for Truth is archetypally the spiritual warrior. The spiritual warrior is not aggressive. The spiritual warrior, however, is extremely fierce if you challenge him. Within ourselves, sooner or later we get confronted, and we have to find within ourselves the strength to stand up and defend Truth, which is not an act of aggression. It is an act of assertion, and it's an act of confirmation. If suddenly somebody comes and starts destroying your world or destroying your people or destroying your country, then, out of love, one defends against undue aggression, huh? It would be Bush's responsibility. In fact, his oath of office would require that he support the Constitution and that he defend the life of Americans when they are under attack. That's his Constitutional commitment, and I think he would be a spiritual failure not to do so. Let's just see if that's so: "The president's commitment, which he has taken an oath, is to defend the American people against undue aggression-resist." [True.] He's under oath to do what he is doing, and he would be quite in error not to do so, to defend the innocent. So, someone is attacking your home and your family or your children, then, you ethically and spiritually are entitled to defend that which is being attacked.

You remember when Jesus chased the moneychangers out of the temple. I always wondered what that meant. You mean he was angry and had a fit or something? Didn't seem like Jesus to me would have a fit about the thing. No. But he came into it out of his spiritual warrior and said this is nonintegrous. And it's a desecration of what the temple stands for. So, he was like defending the Truth, you understand what I'm saying? That explained it, so that was the first time I really understand what he was about there. He was sort of like indignant about the desecration. Like each of us feels a certain indignation that the innocence of these, probably extremely devoted, Muslim boys is being raped and taken over by that which is nonintegrous and telling them lies and getting them to destroy themselves in service to that which is the opposite of Love and Truth. All of us feel a certain indignation about it.

You can take any young child and brainwash them, and they'll end up believing anything. Anybody who has seen things on the History Channel about life in Hitler's Germany remembers how the children were carefully brainwashed in childhood. They couldn't believe anything else except what they believed. So, their innocence, their intrinsic innocence, is taken advantage of. On the other hand, you have to defend yourself against them, you understand. You don't have to make somebody wrong to defend yourself against them. Out of innocence they can run you over.

The Pathway of Love

Out of innocence they can kill you. So, you have to take self-protection. So, that's how I see Bush. He's obligated to defend the country against that which he considers to be an attack.

The other thing about politics is because what we know about politics only comes through the media. What comes through the media has been strained, mangled, distorted, and twisted and decided, and you don't know what the truth is, so you can't really have a political opinion because you don't know what the political facts really are. I've been in circles back east where, over lunch like it was nothing at all, great barons of industry and finance would say, "Oh, come on, a quarter of a point, yeah, a quarter of a point." The lives of millions of people have just gotten screwed. A quarter of a point across 50 million people; you're talking about billions; you know what I'm saying. Does the public know that went on? No. Do we know what Bush knows about the international situation? We don't know what it is. Do we know what the Secret Service knows? We don't know what anybody knows. So, our opinions are already manipulated by the media, you see.

The media are constantly manipulating. The news broadcast is constantly manipulating it. For instance, just by how many seconds they give to one scene rather than another scene, you know? Over on one side, they'll show you all the wounded Palestinians dying there. On the other side, they show you all the wounded Israelis dying there, and there's always the dead baby and the crying mother, always. That really rips people up; that's the old guaranteed one, always the mother with the dying baby. Which side you give the most seconds to is the way you influence the minds of the populace. The "collective minds of the populace" is like a musical instrument, and the media merchants know how to play it—nothing to it. The whole populace is playable. You can just play them this way or play them that way. Give them a few more seconds this way, and you will see the votes go up. Give it a few more seconds this way, and the votes go down. The real maestros of the media play the public like a musical instrument. Any kind of music you want—or this side, any kind of music you want. We can get any kind of music we want out of public sentiment by political manipulation. This is all unconscious. Most people, don't forget, are unconscious. Spiritually aware people start seeing through these illusions and the brainwashing of it, to believe in certain beliefs. So, we can't really judge what goes on, because we don't know what goes on. Who knows what goes on in the secret rooms? As I say, I've been in clubs that were so exclusive, the world doesn't even know they exist. And their decisions are made just like willy-nilly that affect the lives of millions. Nobody gets to vote on it. Your mortgage rate just goes up, that's all. And you didn't get to vote on it. The Congress didn't get to vote on it. The president didn't even get to vote on it. Nobody got to vote on it.

[Q]: "Can a person reach the level of 600 without passing through the 500s? And if so, must I then go back and backfill the 500s?"

That is a cute question. You find yourself up at 600 and say, "Oh, man, I forgot the 500s! I got to back there and shovel some more dirt and earn my chevrons." No, the peculiar thing about it is, you see, context is so complex, it's not comprehensible. That's the wisdom of surrendering all judgmentalism to God. Because the reality is so profoundly complex, it's only when you see it you realize it's staggering. It's *profoundly* complex. Everything that ever existed anywhere in existence, throughout all of what we call "time" is influencing subtly and powerfully every single decision, thought, choice. Every place you put your foot is already the result of the entire universe throughout all of time to make the decision to use that as a demonstration to this audience right at this moment. Where the thought came from is already the result of billions and trillions and multiquadrillions of events, circumstances, influences, etc.

This also, as we will get to next time, goes on through whole sequences of time and events. The beginning of the evolution of consciousness in the universe, throughout all of time, then through the animal kingdom, then up through mankind, and then dissolution of the ego. So profoundly complex, then, one can suddenly jump from almost any level, up to an extremely high state, for reasons unknown. I always tell people, when you start going into bliss states, when things start to suddenly look beautiful—you're driving along, and all of a sudden everything is like in incredible technicolor, you say, "God, everything's beautiful!" Profound stillness seems to prevail over all things, and Light starts to come from within yourself, and you realize that's who you are—it's time to let your friends know that you're spiritually very serious. Because someday, while in the middle of a bagel, you'll suddenly get blissed out, and they call the doctors. Is he catatonic or blissed out, or what?

Satchitananda, you know, can be very paralyzing. I've been in it, and you cannot function; there's no desire to function; whether the body falls over and dies, so much the better; you couldn't care less. It's not a reality. And if you still have an attachment to love, not Love itself, but an attachment to love, you may come back into the body and resume life.

You see, you can go there from the pits of hell. In this experience here, it was at the pits of hell. It must have been lower on the bottom of the Map. The pits of hell are down below here. I don't want to scare people and tell them what it's like there. But anyway, you can go from the pits of hell up to an extremely high state and bypass all of it. Why is that? Because the ego's not a reality. You don't have to undo that which doesn't exist. You just have to bypass it. You don't have to disassemble the ego, because it's only illusion that keeps it in place. You can go up hundreds and hundreds of points in an instant. Well, it isn't just an instant, but all of a sudden, the landscape changes and one's reality changes, sense of who you are changes, and one has just transcended all of it.

THE STATE OF SATORI

Now, that state may not last. In the beginning, spiritual workers get discouraged because they'll go into a really great state, and then it disappears. That's the "black night of the soul." Christian saints, a number of them have written about it. "Oh, woe, Lover, why have you left me destitute and in blackness and despair?" Because the Presence is so exquisite that should it leave, you feel a tremendous sense of loss. So, in the beginning, these states may come but not

KARMA AND DEVOTION

stay. They may come and disappear and come and disappear. But each one sets a different level of what's possible, even though in the beginning it may not stay. This is common in Zen meditation. You can go into a state of satori, and then it leaves you when you get up and walk around the room. In fact, in Sanskrit, classically these various states have been well calibrated over the years in the Hindu tradition.

There are states where in meditation you go into an extreme state, but then when you get up and walk around, it disappears. There's extreme states, let's say, in the beginning that only happen when your eyes are closed, then you lose them if you open your eyes. Then, as you get more advanced, the states of samadhi persist even though you open your eyes. Then, as you get more advanced, the state of samadhi persists even though you get up and begin to walk around; get up and walk around, and that state continues. Then there are states beyond that, which are permanent, and nothing affects it. They are permanent, but you can't function. Then, there is probably the ultimate state in which it persists, and yet you are able to function again. Nothing you do changes the inner reality. It is that which is clear and obvious beyond all time, and that which you are is very obvious and clear beyond all time. But, by forcing one's attention on a detail, you can force yourself to see what is out there. Ramana Maharshi described that and it may have been useful in refunctioning in the world.

If you focus your consciousness on the outer world, you're more able to function there. And then you can withdraw it, and all the energy goes back into the Self. So, how to balance all energy being in the Self, which may be incapacitating, and all energy being in the world is a matter of learning.

So, let's have the mantra to remind us of the purpose for which we're here today. Because the mantra, Om Namaha Shivaya, at 740, automatically puts you there, where the exquisite beauty of the world shines forth. Then one sees the divinity of all that exists. The expression of all that exists is God manifesting Himself as that which you are.

The Pathway of Love

[Q]: "What is the one thing you still want in the world?"

The ego's illusion is, if you don't want it, you won't get it, you know what I mean? The wanting it is what gets it for you. So, the way I prevent it is I keep wanting it, which prevents it from happening in my life, and then I won't be attached to it.

THE FINAL RUN: FIXITY OF ATTENTION

In talking about spiritual work, there are some things I think about, you know, that I should have said. One is, when you're making . . . it's like the energy of spiritual work keeps getting stronger and stronger. Finally, one decides to really go for the final run, you know what I'm saying? What that really consists of is a fixity of attention, a relentless staying with it. Let's see how I'm not expressing that correctly verbally. Some people say, "Well, I've done spiritual work on and off for thirty years, and I'm still where I was." Well, they've meditated a little there, they pray a little there, they go to a workshop there, they hear a speaker there, they read that. It's all sort of sporadic. That's all right when you have time. Let's say you're quite a bit in the world, and you're accumulating data that you know you are going to use at a later date. Certain understandings, certain comprehensions come about.

But then there comes a time when it means to do whatever practice you're doing without exception, *all* the time. A very high state can arise, in temporal time, rather briefly if one is committedly persistent. The devotion to the truth becomes overwhelming. The love for God pulls you. It isn't that you're driving it; it's now you're being pulled by your own destiny. By one's own karmic commitment, let's say, you've chosen the ultimate destiny. Now that begins to pull you and attract you. It isn't that you're being driven by it; it's that you're being pulled by it because that's your destiny. My guess would be that's the destiny of everyone here; otherwise they wouldn't be here.

Then comes a time for becoming really very serious about it. At that point, let's say you use the technique that I used the most was surrendering and letting go of everything at the very moment it arises. So that what arises in consciousness is like a wave. It's like 1/100th of a second; it's coming, it peaks, and then it leaves. So, the letting go-ness is at the peak of it. So that one is constantly like floating over the waves. In other words, all these thoughts begin to arise, and you intuit their intention, and you already release that intention—surrender everything to God. So, this becomes continuous, continuous, nonstop. I remember trying to let go of a severe attachment, and for 11 days I sat and did nothing but let this go. Every thought, every feeling, every memory, everything as it arose was surrendered. See, because the energy behind some thoughts has accumulated through many lifetimes. The grief that you feel when you lose a member of your family now is not just due to losing this person here and now. It's from all the deaths of all the lifetimes accumulated as an accumulation of energy. So, when you begin surrendering that, you may pull up a major, a major one that's accumulated through many lifetimes.

This particular one, as I say, was nonstop for 11 days, morning and night, just went on and on and on and on. And finally, it stopped—gone forever. Never again will you be subject to that. Then arises the next one, so, serious spiritual work is a continuous willingness to let things go as they arise, in the technique that I share. The letting go and the willingness to surrender wanting to control everything as it arises. The willingness to surrender wanting to change it, have it your way, the refusal to surrender it to God.

Very often, one has illusions about the nature of reality. They have to be let go also. That there's a good and a bad; there's a desirable and undesirable—that's all in your mind. So, you realize that the sun shines, and then the clouds come up; and then the rain falls, and the grass grows up and dies; the stock market goes up and down. Age comes and goes. People arise and leave. So, you see, there's the ebb and flow. And if one is at this part of the cycle, there's no point in crying about it, because the cycle will cycle itself out, you see. And by surrendering one's self to whatever's cycling up is how one disappears it eventually. You disappear it by choosing to be with it and letting go wanting to change it as it arises.

To do that particular technique means to do it continuously, no matter what, nonstop. Usually, one can do a run for a period, and then of course, when you get more adept at it, to go back into the ultimate state takes about an hour of releasing all the things that have been accumulated, and then the state takes over. But then you are immobilized in functioning as far as the world is concerned, you see. But you know it's close by, and let's say, a wish like wishing to be comprehended and understood by all to whom I am speaking has to be surrendered, because the comprehension of the truth of what I am saying is not up to the speaker. So, those illusions arise, and as they arise, you let them go. The comprehension of what is being said is up to God, and *what* is being said is up to God, and there isn't any person saying them in the first place, so there's no person who wishes you should get it better. But you can see old ego habits arise, you know.

* * *

So, then, when one surrenders everything that stands in the way of the Presence, the Presence is so obvious, so startling, and so overwhelming that there's no question about it. It is profound, it is total, it is all-encompassing, totally overwhelming, totally transforming, and completely unmistakable, completely unmistakable—that's the minor understatement of the world.

So, I wanted to make that clear, that you can't complain that spiritual work hasn't worked for you, because it's a profound commitment. If you're doing *A Course in Miracles*, let's say, it means you've got to forgive everything all the time, continuously, no matter what. Doesn't mean you can make an exception here and exception there, you know. It means, continuously, because the one or two things you hide behind is usually a stack. That's why you hang on to it. It's not just this SOB you hate; it's a whole stack. And so, all of that hides behind this one, so it's not just an innocent, "Well, I think I'll skip my ex-mother-in-law." Nah, she was adorable . . . and you see her for what she is.

CHAPTER 2

Fields of Consciousness

The value of humor. Humor is also a spiritual technique, because what humor does is you enlarge the context to the point that it disappears polarities. Seeming opposites dissolve; the comic dissolves what seems like the opposite ends. So, comedy and tragedy, winning and losing, all become one and the same. And it's humorous, you see. Humor is another spiritual technique whereby you dissolve the seeming polarity of the opposites, which also are an illusion, but in so doing. . . . So, as you get closer and closer to a really high state, you can't stop laughing sometimes; I mean everything is funny, you know.

So, someone said here, but as you get near a state of Joy. . . . Isn't that this question here? No, that's a different one. As you get near a state of joy, she starts to cry, and crying is a signal of the onset of a certain state of consciousness. The crying is not out of sadness. The crying is out of a joy, but it's a tempered joy. It's not the Joy of high Ecstasy. So, these are different levels, and in some other writing I do, I try to discern the various levels.

A PEACE BEYOND DESCRIPTION

Ecstasy is something different. Ecstasy is an ecstasy in the Presence of God which is beyond description. An extreme Ecstasy and extreme Joy. So, the states of Lovingness, Bliss, Joy, extreme Ecstasy—How do they resolve themselves? Because you can't really live in that state. You can't really live in this dimension in that state. So, what is the resolution of these states? The resolution is, one surrenders the joy, the ecstasy, because the rule is: everything is surrendered to God. You surrender the joy, the bliss, the ecstasy. That may not even come to you for a couple of weeks. Suddenly, like a knowingness is to surrender even the joy. And when the joy and the ecstasy and the exquisite bliss is surrendered to God, then comes the ultimate state. A peace beyond description. A peace of such dimension it transforms all that exists into an infinite and profound peace, the peace of God, which is beyond all understanding. Then, there is an inner quietude which is imperturbable, no matter what happens. So, that is the ultimate resolution of the high states in which emotions are still pulled in, whether it's joy, ecstasy. The willingness to surrender that state requires the resolve to be willing to let go of happiness, joy, and an infinite ecstasy for God, is a great demand. Unless one has acquired that skill, it's unlikely going to happen. Because it is dazzling beyond all imagination, and to think that one has to let this go seems unthinkable. But, beyond it is something even greater—the profound peace of God, which is beyond all understanding, is the ultimate.

[Q]: "Can people below 200 find accurate answers to questions?"

Yeah, ask somebody who's over 200. There's nothing magical about 200. This is integrity. Integrity is the willingness to tell the truth about yourself and about all things to the best of your ability, to be responsible. The difficulty with a psychopath is even when you've got him fingerprinted, you've got the DNA, and you've got a videotape on him, he sits there and says, "I didn't do it." It's profound; you see it on television all the time. They've got DNA all over the place, all over the body, all over the walls, all over his car, they've got a photograph of him, they've got his fingerprints, and he says, "I didn't do it." What can you say about that? What can you say about that? "They're possessed by lower astrals-resist." [True.] Thank you. The reason why the person says, "I didn't do it," they didn't—lower astrals did it. You see them all the time on TV. And many times, these criminals who kill many people will say, from a certain level of truth, "I didn't do that." If he means his ego, no, he didn't do that, but the entity that prevails within has taken over his consciousness. For some reason, then, if you deny the Truth, you're not allowed to access the Truth. It's like you can't have the benefits of honesty without being honest. So, I think that's the answer to that.

The most important thing you want to know about any teacher or entity that channels from the other side—somebody asked me about a teacher on the other side—the name begins with K. That teacher is over 350 or so; 350 then. 350 is very intelligent and integrous, so that's a very good teacher for a certain degree. When you outgrow a teacher, you sort of sense that you're outgrowing the teacher, and you look for somebody, for something, or some teacher that's somewhat higher. It isn't the height of the teacher. It isn't the calibrated level. It's the suitability for yourself, suitability. Because, otherwise, what the teacher is saying doesn't make any sense to you. If you say this teacher doesn't make any sense at all, that's probably the wrong teacher because. . . . If you are at one level and the teacher is there, they will make sense to you. But if you're down low, and the teacher is way up here, you may say you can't really make sense of it. So, we have to decide what's best for us at a certain time. Sometimes, kinesiology is useful for that. Say, "This teacher is good for me at this time." Yes, no, right. And that teacher is good for you right now.

[Q]: "Is the level of consciousness one will reach in this lifetime predestined?"

I would say no, because choice is always present. The consciousness level that you enter life with at birth is already preset by your karmic inheritance. What happens to you during this life is not predetermined innately. However, the circumstances that you find yourself in, the local conditions, will certainly influence what choices you make. So, there is a certain karmic spillover, you might say. However, you can go from the depths of hell to the highest states. So, I think the answer is correct. "You're not constrained by any predetermination-resist." [True.] That's true. No, you're not constrained by any predetermination. You are not limited in any way. You start surrendering things as they occur: every feeling, thought, idea, positionality, and perception, and you can escalate very, very rapidly. You can go up 150 points in one lecture.

[Q]: "When you do kinesiology, do you check for unconscious blocks?"

Well, yes, you can have an area that's obscure. You can pray about that. I ask God to reveal to me, you know, what is the meaning of that, what is the context which makes this seem to be true to me? And you can also use kinesiology, and you can also do karmic research.

The sound of "Ah." The book by John Diamond, *Your Body Doesn't Lie*, the hero of kinesiology, has to do with the sound "Ah." The sound "Ah" is different than the sound "Om." And as we pointed out in one lecture, considerably different from "Aum." The sound "Ah" makes you go strong with kinesiology. So, if you feel blown out, upset, and disturbed by something, you know—the thymic thump—you go hahaha, hahaha, hahaha! That activates the thymus gland, which controls the acupuncture system. It tends to take you out of a negative field and back into a positive field.

A person may not do well with kinesiology if they've been listening recently to music that calibrates quite low. There are certain rock groups, for instance, and they use it for background, and you're watching the advertisement, and you don't realize that the energy of the music in the back is what's blowing out your acupuncture system right now. And you will get a false negative. That particular exercise—hahaha, hahaha, hahaha, at the same time you picture something or someone you love—will straighten you back out again. The effect of negative advertisements, sound, music. One was recently on the news. Pepsi Cola was contracting with some rock singer or something like that, and I think it was Bill O'Reilly got teed off about it and raised hell about it. Anyway, Pepsi Cola let this guy go. Well, let's see what the energy of that enterprise would have been. "We have permission to ask the energy of that particular kind of music-resist." [True.] "It's below 100." [True.] "Below 90." [Not true.] "It's about 95." [True.] About 95. So, you see, if you advertise a product and you put on music

Fields of Consciousness

that calibrates at 95, what you're doing is destroying your customer base. Because that association is made unconsciously.

So, on the other hand, "Ah" and the sound "M," so "Amen" has both of them. Let's go with "Ah." "'Ah' makes one go strong." [True.] "'M-mmm' makes one go strong." [True.]" "'Ommmm' is over 700." [True.] "'Om' is over 720." [True.] "'Om' is over 740." [True.] "'Om' is over 750." [True.] "'Om' is over 780." [True.]

The sound "Om" is very high. The sound "Ah" makes you go strong with kinesiology, and that's why Dr. Diamond uses "hahahahaha." So, we've done it in fact in groups, because I've given lectures on consciousness and kinesiology for many years. We had groups at Sedona; there was a rehab place for alcoholism, and a very excellent one too. About 20 beds, and we would do this with the group. People would come in blown out by their drugs and alcohol and rock music and all that stuff. First, they would be weak. We'd ask them something true, and they would go weak with Truth. Uh-oh. Then we would have them do these exercises, and now they would go strong with Truth and weak with falsehood.

The difficulty with certain kinds of music is that it reverses the field. That which is, you know, if you listen to certain rock groups, now you will go strong with that which is truly wicked, and you will go weak with that which is divine. So, there is a very serious problem affecting the youth, you know. It is the main channel in which the consciousness level of youth is being undermined. It is coming through the invisible soundless vibration that goes along with such music. The world thinks it's the lyrics; it's not the lyrics. The lyrics are bloody and horrible, but even without the lyrics, the energy that accompanies the music is demonic, you might say, and its effect on human beings—it makes them go weak with Truth and strong with that which is false.

[Q]: *"When people go through* A Course in Miracles, *by lesson 75-90, the normally noxious stimuli, like artificial light, etc., no longer make one go weak. What is the reason for this?"*

Oh, well, according to the *Course* itself, you are only subject to what you hold in mind. Eventually your own consciousness becomes stronger than the negative influence of what you might call "adverse energies or vibrations." Eventually you come even to fear, for instance. As I said, what would you do if somebody's about to blow you away with a .45, you just wait, because I mean, it's his problem; he's going to have to face the consequences of blowing you away. So, you serve him at the last moment, because as he pulls the trigger he realizes, "Geez, I just made a bad one, bad mistake." He gets that because of your willingness to love him and forgive him even though he's killing you. So, suddenly he wakes up and says, "Wow, that's the wrong way to go." And that's why you grin and smile at whoever is shooting you. Keep them laughing, you know what I'm saying. You've got to keep them laughing, because otherwise he might go to bad places, you know what I mean? We don't want him to go there.

So, as consciousness advances, you're less and less subject to negativity. One reason is, you don't give it any energy; you don't give it any power. And you begin realizing the nature of God is such that the essence and the truth of who you are is unaffected by anything in the world, and the only thing that interferes with it is belief systems. The only thing that has power over you is the beliefs of your own mind. The only thing that has power over you is the beliefs of your own mind. That is the lesson around lesson 75 in *A Course in Miracles*.

This question has to do with aligning one's gifts and purpose with one's spiritual journey. I would say that's the totality of the commitment. You commit all your assets, everything that you're capable of. If you are a good engineer, you dedicate your engineering skills to serving mankind in whatever way, whether it's providing a factory from which people are going to earn a living, and life is going to then be supported by it. So, you surrender whatever skills you have—music or art, whatever your talents may be.

Fields of Consciousness

Teaching, you teach the children, but you're teaching them from a certain energy, which is a. . . . So, it's the context from which you are teaching the children, not just the content. Because there are some teachers that inspire you, and there are other teachers that discourage you. There are teachers that are very traumatic. You can have a teacher in grade school that takes years to recover from, right? Many years to recover from, I mean a horrendously horrific teacher.

[Q]: "You talk about surrendering to God. If in nonduality there is no separation or separate 'this' or 'that,' then what is the God that we are surrendering to or being devoted to?"

You can't answer that question without begging the question. What is the "what" of God-ness? That's very good. We'll have to reidentify the nature of God. We did the nature of God, I think—Wasn't it last time that we went through 10 statements, and as a group we all did kinesiology? God is, um. . . . So, we will have to go through the levels of God. God is ultimately what you define God as, in language. Experientially, out of the Unmanifest, beyond all form, the infinite potentiality, which is totally and completely unlimited, is described classically as the Godhead. Out of the voidness, it says in Genesis, out of the non-form arose the manifest as a consequence of the Creator, whose essence is that which creates, and which is continuously present. It is out of the potential, the infinite power that it takes to bring existence out of nonexistence. So, both existence and nonexistence are points of view, positionalities. There is neither existence nor nonexistence. There is only the point of observation, but that is about 850. It's not a problem until you get around 850. Do I exist or not exist? Well, I'll tell you. Stop asking the question, and it solves itself. "Oh, yeah, right." Anyway. I would imagine the person is talking about it experientially. There is a level at which the infinite reality is experienced as "nothingness." It's very profound. It's very overwhelming. Let's calibrate the Void. "We have permission to calibrate the Void." [True.] "It's over 900." [True.] "920." [True.] "960." [Not true.] About 960. A very high state, the pathway of negation. The Buddhist pathway in which the ultimate reality is called Void is the pathway of negation. At 960, you go into the Void, which is very, very impressive. And, unless one has been made aware in advance, one would think this is the Ultimate Reality. It certainly seems ultimate, until a little knowingness within notices the absence of love. Void of everything. And the absence of love is what tells you this ain't it. It's *almost* it, but not quite it.

As you let go identifying with content, you progressively identify and experience the reality of context, until finally it becomes overwhelming. It's the substrate of consciousness itself.

THE PROGRESSIVE FIELDS OF REALIZATION

Form

Register

Recognition

Watcher/Experiencer

Awareness

Observer/Witness

Light of Consciousness

Manifest as Allness/Self

Unmanifest (Godhead)

You usually start from the bottom and you move up. Form is the ego, linear world of that which you think is real. How do you know that you know that? Because it's registering some place. How does it register? It registers as a recognition. You recognize a thought, a feeling, a form. You call it doggie, kitty, whatever you want to call it. In meditation you then come back from the content of what's being witnessed and realize that there's a Watcher/Experiencer. How do you know what's going on in your mind here? Because there's a Watcher/Experiencer that's already a substrate to the content. There's a watcher/experiencer. Now, the interesting thing is that all this whole phenomenon is going on of its own. And, somewhere along in meditation, you realize there's no "I" doing any of this. There's no "I" that is recognizing form, naming form. There's a watcher/experiencer. Within itself, within awareness, there's an automatic field in which thinkingness, watching, feelingness, is happening of its own. Just like protoplasm bleeds on its own. You don't say, "I think I will bleed from this wound." Protoplasm does it because that's the nature of protoplasm. You stick it; it recoils; it bleeds.

You realize something *impersonal* is going on—that within mind there is a witness, witnessing all, no matter what the content is. The same witness sees "this" movie, same witness sees "that" movie, same witness sees "that" movie. The witness doesn't change from movie to movie. You stop identifying with form; you stop identifying with this phenomenon. Recognition obviously comes out of the past, and you realize that you're the Watcher/Experiencer. And then you begin to look for, "Where is the Watcher/Experiencer coming out of?" It's coming out of a more subtle prevailing field. These are called the "subtle levels" in classic Hindu or whatever spiritual tradition. The "subtle bodies," the subtle bodies. In the physicality of the ego, you start going up through the so-called subtle bodies into the various chakras and the various subtle bodies, and you go into the watcher, the experiencer. And you come to Awareness itself. You realize there's only one constant, no matter what's going on and that's awareness. The content of awareness may shift all the time, but the one basic principle which is operative always is awareness.

How do you know that? You know because observing and witnessing is going on all the time. Awareness is the nature of the observer/witness, and again, it's not personal. It's happening of its own. That which is attending to the lecture is not personal.

It's consciousness itself. It has that quality of registering what's going on. So, it doesn't require a personal "you" at all. The Light of Consciousness, then . . . you begin to look at Consciousness as the substrate of thinkingness, mind, thought, etc. Under the Light of Consciousness, you begin to sense that there is an overall field, and that is the context out of which you experience your own existence. Or experience yourself as existing, which again, is a jump in conclusion. Because reality is that which you are neither exists nor non-exists, because it is actually Unmanifest.

The "whatness" of God—that one *is* the very substrate of consciousness itself. One is the *Source* out of which the substrate of consciousness arises. That which is the substrate of Creation and all that exists is not different than the Self of your own existence. And there's the awareness that that which you are is identical with All That Is. And that's the realization of God as Allness. I don't think we even have that on the chart.

The Ultimate Reality is the Oneness and the Allness of existence. That takes you beyond 960. We said 960 was void, in which the ultimate experiential reality is void, or nonexistence, and then you realize that's an illusion. You transcend all that—you let that go, and you realize that the Ultimate Reality is the Allness. God is the Source of the Allness of all that exists—the very source of existence itself.

If you meditate on existence, if you meditate on the quality of existence itself, you automatically get taken to the question of, and a realization of the source of, existence itself. Not existence as "this" or existence as "that." But the fact of existence. . . . How can that which not exists, suddenly exist? What in the world would have the infinite power to create the capacity for existence itself? The basic evidence for the Presence of God within you is your own existence. Without Divinity, no existence is possible; because, in the beginning there was only the void, the nothingness, and voidness, and there was not—so, that which was before the Allness of the universes was the Infinite Potentiality, which in itself was void. Out of the void arose Creation. And we've already outlined

Fields of Consciousness

how evolution is merely the way in which Creation brings itself into manifestation.

I saw a really interesting program on TV the other night about army ants. You learn all about the ego and human nature and a lot of spiritual information from watching animal programs. The animal programs reveal so much, and suddenly as you're watching an animal program, you get a profound truth about the reality of life itself. But here are these army ants, and they're very ferocious. They're fearsome. There were the 10 most dangerous animals on the planet. Number one was the army ant, more ferocious than the water buffalo, more ferocious than a killer dog, more ferocious; the most ferocious thing on the planet is an army ant. They are *formidable*. The only reason we aren't all destroyed by army ants is they are very much smaller than we are. If they were the same size, there wouldn't be any human beings left, because they eat everything in their pathway. They're built as killers. They've got these big giant things that just squish you to death and pierce you to death. And then they've got killer tails on them, and they are very, very powerful for their size. And they've got giant jaws, so if these don't get you, these will, and they will turn around and sting you and knock you out that way. These army ants are really quite impressive, and they arise by the billions. They eat everything in their path. They eat all living things in their path. And one interesting thing, there's a certain kind of army ant, a soldier ant, whose abdomen.... First of all, these killer ants are very adept at calculating the size of the other army. They can send back scouts and send back signals. And they withdraw. Or, if they are more powerful, the scouts will signal, in which case they attack and destroy the other colony. Unlike people, who often don't know they've lost the war and make you drop another atom bomb on them before they get the point. So, anyway, this particular army ant is a specialist. His abdomen can grow like this, and at the proper moment, at the right time, he explodes. This army ant explodes, and when he does, he spits this inner toxic poisonous chemical that he's held within his abdomen. He commits suicide in order to kill the enemy, and in so doing, brings about, I'm sure, in his own little mind, salvation, right? He gets nine lady ants on the other side.

And you say to yourself, "You know, how does this differ from human consciousness at all?" It doesn't differ at all! It's identical. Identical thinking, contextualization, techniques, even. You blow yourself up to kill the enemy for the sake of your side winning. I mean, this is incredible, isn't it? This little ant knows all this already, and we are just learning it. How can the ant know better than we do? I mean, they know when they are winning and when they're not winning, and when they're not winning, they take off. We hang in until they've slaughtered every last German or whatever, you know. After the war is lost, they throw in more and more legions and soldiers who are then slaughtered into meat. How come the ant knows more than that? I just thought it was interesting, because the evolution of consciousness to see the visible world of life, animal life, is nothing but the out-picturing of that which has already occurred on the level of consciousness. So, evolution is obviously occurring on the level of consciousness. So, this whole paradigm of army and scouts and winning and blowing yourself up against the army already exists on the, you might say, psychic plane. Right? Let's see if that's so. "This pattern already exists on the psychic plane." [True.] "This pattern which I just described is coming from the lower astral-resist." [True.] "Or lower astral pattern-resist." [True.] "Which then manifests through anything that calibrates under 200-resist." [True.] "So, anything that calibrates under 200 is game, is fair game for the lower astral-resist." [True.] Wow! No wonder.

That explains the phenomena of the world. Anything that is not integrous and is not committed to Truth is fair game to be dominated by the lower astral. Therefore, the murderer easily gets taken over because he's just crashed from 200 down to minus something or other, and instantly, he's now fair game for an entity to take over. I see what the whole pattern is. It makes sense. So, we learn a lot about spirituality from watching the animal channel.

[Q]: "How can you raise a child not to develop an ego?"

Well, you can't! You can give them spiritual standards, because, by spiritual standards, unconsciously, if not consciously, the child will then begin evaluating his own behavior. If you're a good parent and loved so that you're incorporated within their psyche—"interjected," it's called in psychoanalysis. You interject the parent. If it's a good parent, that becomes the ego ideal. In Freudian language, the ego ideal is the ultimate of what you want to become. So, if your father teaches you not to flinch in the face of pain, then you develop the capacity to have amputations without anesthesia because this is an ideal that you powerfully energize. So, the parents are setting up our ideals and standards by which the child is conscious as they grow up. We teach them to be kind to animals, to be kind to each other, to forgive instead of retaliating, to try and see that the other person can't help being the way they are—because you can't forgive them if you see them as bad. But you can feel sorry for them as not being able to help themselves and pray for them. We set up these spiritual ideals, which become incorporated within one's sense of ethics. So, I think we do a lot for our children by bringing our own spiritual awareness as something that we strive for. You also want to set up a mechanism whereby the child doesn't feel guilt if they fail to reach that level. This is what we strive for. And we sometimes fail because the nature of the mind and the human brain is that we're not going to win every time. But that's all right, because it isn't whether you win or lose; it's the direction that you go. So, if the child just gets the direction, it is of caring for yourself and caring for others and trying to perfect yourself as best you can; that's going to be an ideal that's going to stay with them. Stay with them all these many years since. So. . . . The beauty of spirituality, the beauty of religion at its highest expression, can stay with you for a lifetime. Just to experience a great cathedral with the full choir and a full orchestra, and the sun coming through the windows, and the beautiful incense, the magnificence of the architecture, the carvings, the obvious reverence of the people, is a profound impact in your psyche, you know? That forever will have an impact. And anything that falls less than that subtly will not be accepted within the mind. You may accept it for 20 or 30 years, but after a while you give it up.

[Q]: "What's the sighting of UFOs all about? And being abducted by aliens?"

"UFOs are primarily perceptual misinterpretations-resist." [True.] "The UFO as commonly defined is an existent reality-resist." [Not true.] No, not an existent reality.

I saw UFOs one time, and I tested it out with kinesiology, and it said they weren't. Darn it! I'll tell you how it came about because it explains how anybody can believe this. Friends were driving in another car. We were going up to First Mesa, up to some Indian reservation. We were going up for the snake dance or something. Anyway, we were in separate cars. I saw two silvery space vehicles or planes or balloons or something. And they were way up in the sky, and they were quite a bit distant, probably 30 miles ahead of us. All of a sudden, they stopped. All of a sudden, they moved sideways. They moved at right angles quickly. I thought, "Good God, what is that?" So, when we arrived at our destination, we got out of the cars, and I said, "Did you see that?" They said, "Yeah." It was big silvery spheres that suddenly moved at right angles. Wow! We thought we had seen UFOs! Only a UFO can go from a standstill, make a right angle, and go somewhere.

Let's just test my personal experience. "They looked like UFOs-resist." [True.] "I semi-believed that they were UFOs at the time-resist." [True.] "They were not UFOs-resist." [True.] So even though you see perception, as I described the perception, you would say, "Well, I don't believe in UFOs, but by God, what were those things?" How could they go at a right angle like that suddenly, out of nowhere? A pair of them, suddenly go off like that. So, you can see how people can easily arrive at the belief that there are such things.

Fields of Consciousness

[Q]: "What about being abducted by aliens?"

"I am susceptible to getting abducted by aliens-resist." [Not true.] "It's possible to be physically abducted by aliens-resist." [Not true.] "It's possible for your astral body to be abducted-resist." [True.] There's where the event is happening. The event is happening; people that see apocalyptic endings of the world and all, you're talking about a different dimension. It's true in that dimension. There was a spiritual teacher well-known here in Sedona, now deceased, who described that he experienced this vision. All his followers prepared for the eventuality—you know, underground houses and the final days and survivalism and all that. The conviction with which he told it was convincing to the listener. But what you don't get is he's describing accurately what went on, but what goes on in a different dimension. Understand that? There are different dimensions. We live in a different dimension. "He was talking about a lower astral vision." [True.] "The same as the book of Revelation-resist." [True.] Talking from the same level, about 70, as the book of Revelation. Throughout history, mankind has reported with great conviction, because it was experiential and real, that such-and-such is true. The only thing they didn't know was that it is not the same dimension as this.

I can have a patient who goes into a state that we would call from our viewpoint a psychotic state, delusional state where all these tremendously horrible paranoid happenings are happening. They are being kidnapped and tortured and killed and all this. And experientially, subjectively, it's a reality to the person. There is no point in trying to talk people out of paranoid delusions. Because you're not going to talk them out of it because their experiential reality *is*, for the same reason you think that I have two legs. You see two legs here experientially, so you say he has two legs. Now somebody says, "He doesn't have two legs; he has only one leg." "I saw two legs." You know what I am saying? The subjective reality is convincing because it *is* an experience—it's experiential. It's not that they're mistaken; it's just that they don't understand that it is a different dimension. There are various ways to access other dimensions. Drugs, all kinds of weird esoteric practices, certain

KARMA AND DEVOTION

tantric practices, they're all designed, whirling around, going into a trance, using various kinds of drugs, shamans, and exercises in sorcery. And in invoking demons, you can begin to explore other dimensions.

If you are seriously spiritually committed, I advise against this strongly. One of them is going to grab you by the ankle and say, "Gotcha!" "Gotcha." "Gotcha." Why? Because these other dimensions have been there a long, long time—longer than humans. The lower astral dimension has been a powerful dimension, longer than mankind. We're just amateurs. Let's see if that's true. "The lower astral preceded mankind-resist." [True.] "And it's been there for millennia, long before mankind arose." [True.] There you go. The other dimensions, the lower astral entities have been kings and gods of their own domains for millennia before mankind even appeared. You're not going to go into their dimension without paying the entrance fee.

That's why I advise people to avoid channeling, because you don't know where it is coming from; you don't know what the intention of the entity is on the other side. You have a hard enough time being able to comprehend the intention and level of consciousness and spiritual integrity of people that are here, visible and in bodies. Can you imagine what you're trying to do with something on the other side, named Joshua, and he's talking to you from ancient mystery schools, and oh my god, give me a break.

I'll give you a magical sign and symbol, you do that, and you'll become an initiate in the mystery school of Bwamhammoha. Right!

All the spiritual truth you ever need throughout this and any other lifetime is already readily available on this planet, because the truth is spoken by every Avatar, every great guru, every great integrous teacher. It's always been the same. And you don't need any other. And the reason you are looking for something else is because you don't want to do what's real. It's a way of escaping legitimate, real spiritual work, is to go off with Guru Baba who channeled the other side and tells you to buy llamas this year and sell them on the stock market or whatever, you know what I

Fields of Consciousness

mean? All this kind of BS. Why would God be of any interest with what you do with your assets and all? Because to God, they aren't even assets. Only you think it's an asset. No. All the truth that's been necessary to know to reach every enlightened state all the way to sainthood and all the way to enlightenment has already been spoken, is already available. Anything else is just an avoidance. Let's see if that's so. "Anything else is an avoidance." [True.] "And a resistance." [True.] "An unconscious resistance." [True.]

So, seeking out that which is not the truth is an unconscious resistance to the truth. Because, to reach the truth, you have got to surrender certain illusions about yourself, and you would rather believe in the mystification from some enchanting Baba on the other side, rather than surrender the fact that you're getting a lot of juice out of being mad at people. You know what I'm saying? Legitimate spiritual work may seem boring and mundane and prosaic compared to the excitement of mystical chants and mystical symbols and mystical inside information and ascending in the hierarchy—which usually costs you a few thousand, each one. You get to go from junior to senior to master to super master. This is 5 grand, this is 10 grand, this is 20 grand, this is 25 grand. So, there seems to be some other motivation.

WASTE NO TIME

There's a question about astral travel. Well, I've already pretty much answered it. "If you want to reach enlightenment, it's best to avoid astral travel." [True.] "Astral travel can take you to an infinite number of realms." [True.] "Each realm is ruled by a demi-god-resist." [True.] "Who is, in turn, ruled by another one." [True.] "In an endless, infinite number of possible dimensions." [True.] You see? Thank you.

See, this is only one dimension, but there's an infinite number of dimensions. Out of the infinite potentiality of everything-ness arises an infinite number of realms. There's an infinite number of realms, of which this is only one. You have enough trouble understanding this one. There's no point in taking on other realms. Each of which is tailored for a different purpose by different entities and in a different context which you don't know. Even if you get entreated to join something from another dimension, remember one fact: that you are not going there. They're in a different dimension. And you're not going to go where they are, so even if you do what they say, you're not going to be one of them, because they are in a dimension which does not include *you*. They've leaked through, you might say. You get that on radios. The purpose of a limiting circuit in a radio. In the old days, if you turn on the radio, you got all the stations from all around Chicago and Milwaukee and Sheboygan in Wisconsin. You have to have limiting circuits. Limiting circuits prevents all these cross channels because otherwise, everything you turn on, you'll get four or five channels. So, these limiting circuits are there to prevent crossing over from one channel to another. So, first master this channel, and then, if you want to go to elsewhere, go ahead. Except when you master this channel, you find there really are no other channels. There aren't any other real dimensions. But that in itself is an illusion. But you've got to then be the master of all dimensions, and to transcend that, you have got to be over 1000. That takes 1200 to realize. First master this dimension and then see if there are any other dimensions and if you want to go there. Then you realize there are no other dimensions because the completion of Allness is all that there is. It is greater than all dimensions.

One could spend an infinite amount of time just exploring one of these alternate dimensions. You can listen to WGN around the clock. You can also get WBBM, you can also get WINS, you can also get WTMJ, and you would see that you would spend an infinity in exploring all the potential dimensions, none of which is necessary. Because the Ultimate Reality beyond all of them is exactly the same. The Ultimate Reality beyond all of them is exactly the same. Let's see if that's a fact. "The Ultimate Reality beyond all dimensions is something I may ask right now." [True.] "Is exactly the same for all-resist." [True.]

So, there is no advantage to any other dimension in which Master So-and-So takes you to this astral realm, where they meet you with somebody else who takes you to another astral realm. There are people in Sedona who have spent their whole lifetime doing that—they're on realm 42, you know what I mean? I've got news for them. You've got only about 999,000 more realms to explore. In the year 5942, you'll get a teacher that says, "Hey, you're chasing your tail." Because as you chase your tail, more dimensions are getting spun off the wheel, you understand? There's an infinite number. And that is the whole purpose of the lower astral—to keep you going round and round endlessly and never becoming enlightened. Because that which hates God has set itself up to distract all that is attracted to God. So, don't forget that as you evolve, you are going to become meat. You're going to become the target. You're going to become that which all that hates God is attracted to and wants to pull out of the game.

So, the upside of love is bliss, happiness, and the awareness that love and God are one and the same. The downside is, when you get into a state of bliss lovingness, you drop your guard. You see everyone as pure and innocent. They're innocent but not pure. Don't forget the sheep in wolf's clothing. When they see that you're a blissful, happy little spiritual warrior, and you're bumbling down the street, you become fair game for every lower astral that would like to pull you out of the circuit, okay? Without seeing them as evil, you just realize you want to decline the invitation. You want to decline the invitation to follow that which is nonintegrous. If it doesn't meet the test of integrity, you know, Jesus said just avoid it. You don't have to fight it; you don't have to go against it; you don't have to denounce it. Just don't go there. Just don't vote for that candidate. And you know who I mean! Nah.

People can be genuine to their own belief systems, except that their own belief systems are delusional; that's the only problem.

AVOID THE LOWER ASTRAL

Something came up about the lower astral. Everything I've learned about it is you don't want to go there. Let me ask that question. Somebody asked a question: *Can you evolve upwards from the lower astral?* "We have permission to ask this in front of this audience-resist."

KARMA AND DEVOTION

[True.] "You have the karmic permission to evolve from the lower astral-resist." [Not true.] That's why you don't want to go there. Remember the Buddha said, "Fortunate are you that you're a human being. Slim are the chances to be born a human because the human has the chance to evolve all the way to enlightenment. Rarer still is the desire to reach enlightenment, and rarer still are those who have heard of enlightenment, being born a human, and have not taken advantage of this golden opportunity. Therefore, waste no time." Waste no time.

You can "waste no time" very simply because as everything arises in the ordinary course of an ordinary life, you just constantly surrender to God. You don't have to be a rocket scientist to figure out how to do that. "Would I be willing to surrender that to God?" Those of you who have done the 12-step programs, the third step is you surrender your life to God as you understand Him. *A Course in Miracles*, all the really basic spiritual programs, many of which calibrate in the 200s to 300s, but they are solid basic stuff. To surrender everything to God, to hold back nothing, to ask God questions to which you don't know the answer, to ask for guidance from the Holy Spirit within you. Ask for a miracle. You can often just tell the Holy Spirit, "I don't get it." All of a sudden you say, "I don't get it," and as you walk out, suddenly you "get it." Very prompt. I don't know, you get very prompt answers a lot of times.

[Q]: "Is there an ultimately best process for releasing, surrendering, etc., everything to God?"

That's the Willingness. We said, the power of Willingness. See, devotion—Love takes many forms. One form it takes is a powerful decision. When you make a decision to say no to that which is nonintegrous, that's really a very powerful step. "I'm not going to go there, and whatever the consequences, I'm not going there." So, commitment, the willingness to let everything go. It doesn't mean you're going to succeed the first time you let go of a certain desire or wantingness or resentment. It doesn't mean necessarily the first time you let it go. We've said because a lot of these things are an accumulation over many lifetimes. We'll get to that next time. A repetitive pattern shows up over *long* expanses of time. This is just one episode. One's life is not this episode. This is just an episode. This is this particular physicality. One's life transcends many physicalities. So, a pattern can persist and persist and persist. As you try to let go of it, it doesn't always let go right away. But the very fact that you were willing to surrender it and that you did actually go through the process is already a karmic merit, so that eventually you're building up, undoing all the negative karmas, and now, all of a sudden, one day you let it go and it disappears. I don't know, they just don't get you mad anymore. You used to fantasize killing them and murdering them and getting even with them. And now, you don't give a rap about them one way or the other.

Like little mice. Mice running around, I think they're cute. One time I'm sure I hated them, was afraid of them, and now I think they are sort of cute. I chase them out; I hate to kill them because then I'll miss them, and they are going to go off in another body elsewhere, but not in my backyard where I can have fun with them, see.

[Q]: "Can you elaborate calibrations beyond 1000?"

Such calibrations are possible. We don't really know where we are going with this. "Such calibrations are now possible." "Do we have permission?" "We have permission to answer the question-resist." [True.]

"It's possible for the physical nervous system to handle something over 1000." [Not true.] "It's possible for the human nervous system to handle consciousness energies over 1000." [Not true.]

Somebody said, "If this lifetime, you came out of the Void, you left the last time in the Void-resist. We have permission on that one." [True.] "The prior lifetime was left in the Void-resist." [True.] Yes. The prior lifetime, in fact, the ultimate truth was voidness, as far as I knew. That's a certain spiritual pathway which is integrous because it's based on a conviction that that is the ultimate truth. And it's based on a mistranslation, I think, of the teachings of Buddha, because it is only really a matter of contextualization.

KARMA AND DEVOTION

The difference between Allness and Nothingness is a very subtle discernment. On a certain level, that which is all thereby becomes nothing, you understand. Because to be something, you have to be differentiated from the rest. To be "All That Is" is, in a way, being nothing, but it is more complicated than that verbalization about it.

The capacity to let things go is, first of all, a matter of practice, a matter of direction, a matter of habit, a matter of willingness, and basically, it's really devotional. So, the underpinning of any spiritual practice is devotion, the willingness to surrender all to God. And that's what gives it its power. With practice, it becomes a habit; with practice it becomes habitual. You let go wanting to change it.

I was talking out back about being stopped by a cop at one o'clock in the morning on 89A. And we were the only ones on the whole highway. Nobody's out there at one o'clock except me and this squad car behind me. I'm looking at my speedometer—I think I'm not more than 40. Now, why is this guy tailing me? Finally, he pulls me over, flashes his lights, and I said, "What can it be?" "You're weaving." "Weaving? What is weaving?" He said, "You're going back and forth over the yellow line." I'm thinking: "We were the only people on the whole highway, what am I going to do—stay in my lane? There's nobody else here but me." So, he says, "Are you drinking?" I said, "No, I haven't had a drink in forty years." So, he says, "You take dope, smoke stuff?" I said, "No." He said, "You willing to take a so-and-so test?" I said, "Sure." He says, "Walk this yellow line." I walked the yellow line. He said, "I don't know; there's still something wrong with you." He's scratching his head. He said, "What do you think is the matter with you?" And I said, "You know, do you want me to be truthful?" He says, "Yeah." I said, "I don't feel like I'm really in my body." He said, "Good God, I've had exactly the same experience."

So, help me, it was an actual experience. I'm surrendering this to God, and if he gives me a ticket, he gives me a ticket, so let it be. He says, "Gosh, I'm really glad to have met you." I told him I'm a doctor and a psychiatrist and all that, and that gave me more firepower. And I told him I go out of body, and if I don't remember to come back in it, I can wander off, because if you're wandering across in the middle of the night, you're not thinking about what you're doing. So anyway, he was greatly relieved. He said, "This has worried me for years. Now I know what it is." I said, "You just will yourself to be back in the body and, bang! You go back." It's terrific, you know. We left the best buddies, shook hands, hugged. So, one sign of being out of your body is, you weave. He was really a nice officer. He really was. He said, "I really had been worried about that." And here he had found somebody he could ask about it, and I said, "You know, it's not connected with your body's space." Which is one problem that you have when you're first going into certain higher states. You don't know where your body is in space. It's very difficult to navigate because that which is the central controller is gone. So, everything you do is oriented from some imaginary space, somewhere in the middle of your head. When that disappears, where you are in space is not all that clear at all. It's still not that clear very often.

[Q]: "What is the difference between love and joy?"

Well, Love, as we said, takes many expressions. Many people are here out of the energy field of Love, and what they do is energized by Love. Joy is a different state. Joy goes beyond Love and lovingness. Love and lovingness, you can live with all the time. It's sort of an evenness that lights up everything. Joy is more intense. Joy is more exuberant, you might say. Its energy is more—sort of swamps you. Joy sort of takes you over. One can be prone to Joy, prone to Joy, without being in that state all the time. You can go from lovingness, Unconditional Lovingness, into Joy, into Ecstasy. We got Ecstasy up there? No. Anyway, as you ascend the scale, you reach sort of sublime states, states that are really sort of sublime. The Ecstasy is beyond description and hard to handle if you're around people. One time I went into a state of Ecstasy and. . . . There's a chapel over here, the Chapel of Something or Other. Huh? Yeah. At one o'clock in the morning, nobody was there. The candles were all lit, and there was this beautiful music playing. And ecstasy reached such a state that the body began to dance with Ecstasy. I was a pretty good dancer. The only possible way to handle it was to give it physical expression. One sort of was danced by the ecstasy of the glory of God as revealed to your own awareness. Ecstatic. Ecstatic. So, one did that to express to God one's joy and appreciation for Divinity. One's joy is that one has been allowed to experience the quality of Divinity experientially within one's own capacity to experience. So, the joy is almost like an exquisite thankfulness that one has been allowed to experience the Presence and one wishes to reflect back the thankfulness and the joy at the revelation, in whatever manner you're able to express it.

So, the only way you are going to escape Joy is . . . beyond Joy is ecstasy, in here is an ecstatic state. I understood what Ramakrishna went into. Ramakrishna described the exact state, and he would go into ecstatic states. Though the Ecstatic is beyond Joy, Ecstatic I never calibrated. Let's see where Ecstatic is. Can we calibrate "Ecstatic?" "Ecstatic spiritual Ecstasy is beyond 540?" [True.] "560?" [True.] "580?" [True.] "585." [True.] "590." [Not true.] 590.

Spiritual Ecstasy is exquisite. Exquisite. And then, just beyond that, as I said earlier in the lecture, just beyond that Ecstatic state, if you surrender the ecstasy to God, then the infinite Peace of God comes. That is beyond all. However, I wouldn't miss the Joy and the Ecstasy on the way. It's rather profound. See, the other thing that happens in certain states is you get to know who else is there, who else has been there, you might say. You get to experience the presence of a rarefied strata, and those who have been there . . . how can we say it? It's outside of time; it's like they're still there. It's like a shared experience because you've transcended temporality. So, to go into the same state as Christ went into or Ramakrishna or any of the great saints—it's like you share the experience with them. It's hard to explain, but there's a commonality of experience in which your consciousness and their consciousness are actually one and the same. So, in that state, one experiences Ramakrishna's ecstasy because his ecstasy and yours are not different. It's all the same.

Fields of Consciousness

There's a point I call the "High Pass," where you get hit by the Luciferic temptation. "All power is yours. Now that you are beyond karma, now that you don't have to answer to anything or anyone, now that you realize there is no adversarial God who will punish you for anything, and now that you are beyond personal karma, all power is yours—own it. All power is yours." Huh! And in that state, you saw exactly who went through and what they said. It's a very high test, and it's very subtly expressed by the Luciferic energy out of which it arises. You realize that Jesus Christ said no to it. You see who else said no to it, because the falsehood is: yes, you're beyond personal karma. I mean, this presentation is not verbalized—it's a knowingness. It's a knowingness. This knowingness comes as a profound temptation. And, uh, what can I say about it? The error is, yes, you're beyond personal karma, but you are not beyond the karma of the infinite Presence of God, whose context is inclusive of all that exists. You're beyond your personal karma, but you're not beyond the karma of God being the infinite context out of which all arises. You're not beyond the karmic realm of God. You're beyond personal karma, but you're not beyond the karma of the universe. So, if you make that mistake, you end up along with Lucifer and his club there—Lucifer Club.

I have already answered the next question. It says, *"As you begin reaching higher states, you become more favorable game for the lower astral."* You become juicier and a nicer plum to haul home. So, you see a lot of gurus that write books that are quite well-known. Everybody still lights candles to them and all. They were in the 500s when they wrote it, but they have gone way down since. "What do the astral beings get out of that?" They get pulling that which they hate and that of which they are jealous back down. It's like crabs. They say, when you put a bunch of crabs in a pail, if one crab starts to get out, the other crabs will pull him back down into the pail. It's for the same reason that anybody who's successful, rich, powerful, etc., becomes fair target. Discrimination is politically incorrect unless you're successful, in which case discrimination and assault and attack and blackmail and everything else can be thrown at you because you are rich and powerful. Right?

KARMA AND DEVOTION

The same laws don't apply now. So, it would be out of jealousy. So, it's jealousy and hatred. "The motivation here is jealousy and hatred-resist." [True.] So, it's jealousy and hatred, see? Don't forget that the lower astral realm gains by the more evil they are, the more they rank. The game of Dungeons and Dragons. Doesn't dragons and dungeons pretty well delineate the lower astral? It's even got the correct esoteric terminology, the names for them.

So, you know, you're a "made" guy when you murder somebody in front of a witness. Now you rank higher in the Mafia, correct? You're just riffraff down there if you just rob banks and steal from honest people—steal cars and all, you're just punks. Now, you're nobody at all until you are witnessed, so somebody can attest to the fact that they saw you murder somebody in cold blood. Now, you've got rank, huh? It's the rank of "badder and badder and badder." The higher the captive you can pull in, now becomes your servant and your vassal, so you gain power by proselytizing and pulling people into your ranks. I believe that's what it's all about. "That's what it's all about-resist." [True.] That's all it's about; it's just the gamesmanship of who can be the most evil and therefore rank the highest.

You know, history shows some profound examples we've seen on television. The Japanese in Nanjing. The, uh, I think it was a Vietnamese soldier bayoneting the infant in the arms of its mother. Took on a new rank. The ultimate cruelty, hardness, the surrendering to the ultimate, and that's how you gain rank there in the lower astral. And when you get there, you find there's people that are far more wicked than you are. And you're not at the top, you're at the bottom, baby. Wait till we tell you what you've got to do to get farther up the ranks. Oh, boy, so you just don't want to go there. So, the lower astral is to keep us from being focused on enlightenment, and they do represent the temptations of the satanic and the Luciferic. So, we answered those pretty well. And those are things we've also written about to make sure people comprehend it.

There tends to be a "goody-goody-ness" about spirituality sometimes that is a form of denial. Because the spiritual aspirant is also a fair target for that which would like to bring it down. And I think every spiritual student should be forewarned. Forewarned that that which is not integrous will certainly seek to pull you out of the game, certainly seek to pull you out of the game, by one temptation or another.

[Q]: *"Is it best to avoid people who are spiritually below integrity?"*

That's what all the spiritual teachers, including the great Christian saints said—to not hang out with such people because they have sort of a collective karma. And just the fact that you are there begins to attract things to it. That's sort of the "broken window" principle, which sociology has discovered. The broken window—this takes us beyond causality. What attracts negativity is the field, see. It's not sequential causation. It isn't that the broken window "causes" something. The negative energy, which is focused there, the attractor energy field which is focused there, brings upon itself the broken window, which again brings upon itself the drug addict, which again brings upon itself the rape, which again brings upon itself the abandoned baby and those addicted to crime.

And it shows, up of course, initially with graffiti and broken windows and trash on the streets. But, you see, it's not "causal." It's not the broken window *causes* the rape or that the rape *causes* the crime or that the crime *causes* the drugs. And then the gangs get into turf wars over who owns the building. I remember the last time I saw Brownsville or the lower Bronx, the South Bronx; it was unbelievable. It was like you say, "This can't be." You drive through the street, and you see where the smoke had come out from all these buildings that have been set on fire. You see where the smoke had come out from the window, and the side of the buildings are all black and covered with graffiti, the streets are covered with filth, people falling over with drunkenness and alcohol and drugs and prostitution openly on the street. And mugging will take place right in front of your eyes. They don't even give a damn if you watch. They will mug somebody right in front of your eyes. You say, "I've got to be making this up." You know what I mean?

KARMA AND DEVOTION

It's like that energy field is pulling to it, itself. So, you see a lifetime where a person is born in a very low energy field; they're born into that kind of neighborhood, to that kind of parents. Unless their energy field changes, awful things will be happening to them throughout their lifetime. So, they're born into miserable conditions here, and now they are in juvenile jail here, and they've got multiple misdemeanors. And then that usually graduates to a felony. So, when we see a person arrested, let's say, everybody gets sad about and politically correct about "three times and out" in California. Now some guy is put away for life now for stealing a pizza. I tell you—he ain't being put away for a pizza. This guy's criminal background goes back to age six. He's got probably 49 misdemeanors. He's got 23 felonies that nobody detected yet. Two times in prison, and you know the third time is going to put you out and you still steal a pizza, that means there is something missing in your frontal cortex, doesn't it? It means you're not very well anchored in reality. It means you can't control your own impulses. No, you've got a disease called "criminality" that compulsively you're going to keep on doing it, because you can't learn from experience. Because you're not afraid of consequences, because you can't control your own impulses, because this has been a lifetime lifestyle. Like the pedophiles I've treated, you know, "I only got busted one time." Then, in therapy you find out he's molested over a hundred kids. The average pedophile I had treated had probably molested at least 50 or 60, up to a hundred kids before he was arrested. So, he's not being arrested for *this* incident. He's got a record going back this time; he just got caught this time.

So, you have to have the whole picture, the whole context. As we've said, the lie is composed of taking content out of context. And one thing you'll see that the media does all the time is warp reality by not telling you what the context was. He got busted for a pizza and what else? And he's stolen thousands of things, literally, going back over his entire lifetime. A chronic thief: How many things do you think he's stolen before he's finally arrested? Hundreds and hundreds. The rapist, how many times have they raped? Dozens of times. The pedophile? Fifty or a hundred times. So, they are not going to jail for stealing this pizza at all. What's the answer? I don't know what the answer is. To keep them isolated from vulnerable people, as far as I know. I don't know what else to do about them. It seems to be an incurable addiction. And I think it comes from the lower astral. "These are lower astrals that somehow have got into physical bodies-resist." [True.] That's a fact, yeah. Because they have no spiritual inclination and no capacity for honesty.

[Q]: "When did Mother Teresa reach her state of bliss? Early in life or late in life?"

Well, we calibrated that her heart is extremely high. Her heart was like 700. "Mother Teresa's heart was like 700." [True.] "It came about as a result of Christian devotion-resist." [True.] It came about as Christian devotion, you know, unswervingly, unswerving devotion to God.

***

The ultimate state is neither attached—neither attraction nor aversion. Neither attraction nor aversion. So, one surrenders aversions and asks to see it differently, the same as you do with attachments. To have an aversion of something is like the reverse of an attachment, so the ultimate state is non-attached. It means you don't have to be detached; you don't have to avoid it. It's okay if it is and okay if it isn't. That isn't as hard to reach as you think it is. See, Neutrality is a pretty released state. There's a teaching which arose in Sedona, or it was actually in New York, teaching how to get to Neutrality. Letting go wanting to change things, control them, make them different, wanting anything from other people, and it takes you right through Neutrality. You know, if you get the job, it's great, and if you don't, you will find one elsewhere. So, it's a state of freedom. And originally, when I learned the technique, it was back east in New York, and it was called "Freedom." And it had to do with letting go attachments and aversions, by letting go wanting to change them in yourself or out in the world. And if you continuously do that, you become quite detached. It's true, you do become quite unattached.

So, all the things that you learn, levels, you know, it isn't that 500 is better than 200—it's not "better than." It's just you're in a different space, like being in a different place on the map. Your problem to get from here to there is different if you start out from Albuquerque or you start out from Denver. You're just in a different place, and therefore, you're looking at different lessons. But you can go from one level quickly all the way up to the . . . so, you can't say that because you are at 200 this week, you can't be at 500 next week. You can be at 500 on the way home in the car. Suddenly, *kshew!* Out of a flash, you just . . . because whatever's blocking it, the minute you let it go, then you open for the Light to come in, and the Light comes right in.

[Q]: "How come a person can go from a really great state to a lousy state very quickly, in a matter of seconds?"

That's called "being human," huh? That's called being at the effect of being a human and having a human brain. And the human brain, as it's constructed, you understand, is an add-on. The prefrontal cortex, that which makes us human, is an add-on to the old animal brain. The reptilian brain is still there; all the basic primitive brains all throughout the eons from 400 million years ago, are still there and still operative; and you know, by choice, you can become an instant killer. The old dragon is still there, and we've learned not to respond to it. But that impulse to kill still comes up, and it comes out of the old amygdala or wherever the hell it is.

Like the Komodo dragon, yeah. We have permission to calibrate his energy. Let's see. "Komodo dragon." [True.] "It's okay to calibrate his energy." [True.] "It's over 20." [True.] "25." [True.] "30." [True.] "40." [True.] "45." [Not true.] About 45. If you get bitten by something that's at 45, you wish you hadn't. Imagine this guy who was a friend of a movie star or something; he goes into the cage with a Komodo dragon—oh my god, I think, with no boots on or something. Anyway, he's still alive.

Fields of Consciousness

[Q]: "So, it's possible for a person to do kinesiology with a reasonable degree of accuracy by oneself?"

See, one thing about kinesiology is you *can*, by asking a question in many different ways if you are doubtful about a question: "If this is so, then that over there must be so." If you ask them independently, you'll get corroboration. So, if I were questioning the level that I got on the Komodo dragon, I would utilize other things that I know about reptilian life and primitive life and primordial life, and contextualize it now in a whole field of data. Then, if it didn't fit the data, I would have to go back in and find out why that is so. What did we say the Komodo dragon calibrated at? 45. So, he's worse than *Tyrannosaurus rex*, huh? "We can do *Tyrannosaurus rex*?" [True.] "He's over 65." [True.] "He's over 70." [True.] "75." [Not true.] *Tyrannosaurus rex* is at 70. The Komodo dragon is at 45. I mean, it's just a curiosity, you know. How do all those creatures line up? I don't want to meet one in the dark.

[Q]: "The ego isn't real, is it?"

That's correct. It's not a reality any more than is mind. Both *mind* and *ego* are general terms. The only trouble with using general terms is people believe if a thing has a name, it must have an existence in reality. That's how a great deal of illusion arises. If we have a name for something, then it must be real. A lot of names are merely tautologies. In other words, it means what you define it to mean. And by common usage, it gains ground, and pretty soon, the mind begins to think it's a reality. The belief in causality is the most serious error in that regard. See, because sequentially, one thing follows another, we now impute from imagination something mysterious within the world called "causality." Well, if you dissect all these things here, you show me "causality." You won't find any because there ain't no "causality" there. "Causality" is within the belief system of the observer. It has no objective independent existence.

This is demonstrated mathematically, of course, in quantum mathematics, quantum mechanics, where what you find is what you look for. What you discover is based on intention.

Whatever your intention is, is what you are going to come up with, because you just defined it. By defining it, you are obviously going to select what you've already defined. So, in other words, a pseudo-objectivity tends to reify itself. You know what *reify* means: It's when you believe in the reality of something that exists only in your mind. When you look out there, you think you get verification of its existence. So, you get a self-feedback amplification of nonreality. Which makes the so-called *ego* difficult to overcome.

"Before we started the lecture today, they were over 435." [True.] "436." [Not true.] "Before we started, we started at 436?" [True.] "437." [Not true.] "The group after the end of the lecture today went up over four points." [True.] "Five points." [True.] "Six points." [True.] "Seven points." [True.] "Eight points." [Not true.] Seven points. "The group went up today seven points." [True.] "Eight points." [Not true.] Seven points. The average lifetime is five points, so you went up over one lifetime just in today. It isn't just the calibrated level, you see, because we're looking at a certain fallacy of logic. It would seem like a moving from a certain point to a certain point. We're superimposing an artificiality, see. To eliminate through a subtle understanding a source of something that's been painful all your life, the payoff is enormous. You understand what I'm saying? Even the most subtle shift of awareness about something, now it no longer has the power to injure you or harm you or aggravate you or make you think about suicide. Now, it's a joke. The difference between tragedy and a joke makes all the difference in the world, eh? So, recontextualizing things may only calibrate numerically at a certain time, but those are germinal ideas. Those are germinal ideas.

So, one germinal idea may only change your calibration one point, but then, because it's been planted, now it's going to transform of its own nature because your intention is superimposed upon it. So, your intention will be more important than whether you went up a few points or something like that. What you do with it, how you value it, and where it grows from there. These things become germinated, and then. . . . You've all had the experience; you're driving down the road, and all of a sudden you "get"

Fields of Consciousness

a complete understanding of something you've heard for years. Suddenly you *get* it. That's a joyful moment. It's like whatever was blocking that awareness is removed now.

Certain spiritual information is, in and of itself, transformational. Let's see that. "Certain critical information is, in and of itself, transformational-resist." [True.] "Some of what was said today is transformational-resist." [True.] So, in other words, all we did, we saw how it shifted the blocks, but then that's going to continue and bring a cascade. So, that's a lot to assimilate. It can also be upsetting to try to assimilate too much, too fast. In a way, you have to, like, grow with it and let it sort of settle, and then you're ready to move on to the next point. And then you're ready to move to the next point. If you jerk somebody right out of one of these patterns here and throw them into another one, it can be very disruptive. Very disruptive. Okay, so each person grows, then, at the rate of their own capacity, their own intention, their own readiness, their own karmic ripeness. And each of us evolves at a specific rate. You don't know what that rate is because, as we've said, the present has already been determined by the future. That's a comfortable thought, isn't it? "Everybody here is being pulled by that star, the infinite power of enlightenment; that's a fact." [True.] "This entire audience is being pulled here because they're destined for enlightenment-resist." [True.] Isn't that amazing? That's a knowingness that I never checked with calibration. Otherwise, there would be no reason to be here, you understand.

The spiritual work is quite strenuous. It's quite difficult at times. It's very uplifting. The overall context is uplifting, but then what that pulls up into the direct focus of your awareness can be sometimes painful and difficult and bring up temporarily guilt and negative feelings. Don't forget, our consciousness evolved over the ages, over the eons. Came up through, as far as we can trace it, the animal world, the reptilian world, on up through the mammalian. And what you pull up out of the unconscious, then, you can spot where its origin was back in time and stop beating yourself up with guilt. Jealousy arose long before you hit this planet. You can watch any monkey colony, and you'll see jealousy right and left—"This is mine! This is mine!" Fighting for the alpha male position, the alpha female position. Joining up in groups, this group, "us" against "them." Once you see its origin, then, you stop attacking yourself.

It's not personal; part of one's karmic inheritance as a human being is to inherit that configuration of instinctual reflexes that we call "ego," but they are really animal instincts. Everything about the ego, you can spot in the animal kingdom, and you can see where it arose—with the exception of quantum mechanics, which did not arise in the animal kingdom. Well, we beat them out there, didn't we? Take that, monkeys and zebras! We had fun calibrating various animals—zebras and kangaroos, and so it's a lot of fun to calibrate the energy field of all these animals. What were the ones we did with the long necks? Giraffes. Didn't we say giraffes were 170? "Giraffes are at 170." [True.] "175." [Not true.] Giraffes are 170. Isn't that interesting? That's higher than a lot of people on the planet, isn't it? You're better off being a giraffe. I mean, you wander around there, and you eat from the trees, and you mind your own business. And a giraffe doesn't give you a problem unless you start attacking them. If you attack a giraffe, he'll give you a whop with his hoof and send you flying. That's a pretty nice way to be, just wandering around and eating from the trees, and you don't bother anybody, unless a lion. The lion has a hard time with the giraffe, because the giraffe is really going to get annoyed by a lion, so. . . . But it's interesting just to calibrate different groups of animals, because you see and begin to recognize in yourself where that all came from. Within you is the happy vegetarian who just likes to munch from the trees and not be bothered with people. In you is also the tiger. You push me far enough, and *wham!* And I'm gonna pull out my claws. So, you see the origin of all of that.

Seeing the origin of it then removes it from personal identification. You realize it's the source of the consciousness which you now call "me," but its origin, you did not devise that. Lions were around; the tiger was around before you got here.

Fields of Consciousness

[Q]: "Do we have spiritual buddies that we like to hang out with?"

We all got spiritual pals we've been hanging out with probably for lifetimes. Let's see, we'll ask. "We've got people with whom we are spiritually aligned for lifetimes-resist." [True.] "Sympatico." [True.] "Buddies, like." [True.] "Friends." [True.] "We are all in the boat, together, kind of thing-resist." [True.] Yeah. We're all in the boat together.

You see, the love for each other creates the field, and then we are attracted to reincarnate in that field because in a way, we're sort of evolving with the field, you know what I'm saying.

A question always comes up about soul mates and their relationships, marriages, whatever. I don't know really what that means—a "soul mate." I don't know if it is a legitimate question or a romantic fantasy. I don't know what "soul mate" really means. "Well, there can be a commitment between two people that transcends reincarnations-resist." [True.] "That can extend over many lifetimes." [True.] Yeah, there can be a commitment between people that extends over many lifetimes. And often, when you run into them again in this lifetime, you feel a state of great joy, you know, *whoosh*—you feel a flash, like recognition. It's not conscious; it just comes up of its own, like a feeling of joy, a spontaneous feeling of joy, of mutual recognition.

"We can ask this one question about people over 700." [Not true.] No. We'll do that another time. It's in the book, anyway. It's in the book. But we did go back over the figures—they had changed because. . . . Oh, yes, there was one question I wanted to answer. And then, we're going to have to quit. "The consciousness level of mankind, I have permission to ask in front of this audience-resist." [True.] "Is now over 206." [True.] "207." [True.] "208." [True.] "209." [Not true.] 208. Since I did . . . it was 205, right? It went up to 207. Anyway, in the last year or two, it has gone up from 207 to 208. Somebody mentioned they felt a shift of consciousness, and we had already detected that.

You know the spiritual work we do on the nature of consciousness itself, don't forget, you are affecting context, not content. See, spiritual work designed to affect content is limited in its power.

Spiritual work designed to advance the field of consciousness itself lifts all the fish in the bowl. Understand what I am saying? You're just trying to affect specific fish. So, a lot of spiritual work, prayer groups, and all, are very well-intentioned, but they really don't impinge what's happening in the world because they're too localized—we're going to pray for peace in Persia or something. You know, that's very localized, very limited. To work towards the advancement of consciousness itself, you know, lifts the whole game, and then whatever content is going on is lifted by the fact that the whole game is being lifted. I think if you just sit around all day praying for peace in Palestine or something, you are probably wasting your time. First of all, they don't want it. "That's a fact-resist." [True.] Right. No, the payoff from hatred and being victim and martyr and getting even and revenge and all, that's a fierce game, and it's very hard to pull out of it. It's very hard to pull out of it. The viciousness is that the one side sets up the other side in such a way that they can't pull out of it. After you've victimized enough children from this side, how are they going to get out not avenging a whole school of children purposely destroyed? So, what you do is trap the other side into "having to" come back at me. You know what I'm saying? It's really vicious because it's poisoning the well, and it's a purposeful intention to prevent anything like peace from arising and being taken seriously. You create enough horror and hatred—you make sure the other side hates you enough. That's really a lower astral trick, to make sure that sufficient hatred has been engendered to ensure the ongoingness of the conflict.

[Q]: "Are there any examples in history where that condition has existed that some sort of intervention has changed it, that you know of, and what might that have been?"

I don't know. All I know is we can track the level of consciousness of mankind as a whole throughout time, and if we had enough study groups, we could do it continent by continent, country by country, culture by culture, and see where it made major changes, and then go back in history and ask which of these things had an effect. It isn't necessarily a cause and effect; it's a matter that certain conditions favor certain moves, see? So, instead of causality, what you see is that certain conditions are favorable to certain potentialities. The quantum potentiality is favored. Rain and sunshine don't *cause* the plant to grow, but they increase the potentiality and the likelihood that the germination will be successful under these conditions. A plant is not *caused* to grow by sunlight; it is not *caused* to grow by light or *caused* to grow by moisture. Those are only the conditions which increase the statistical probability of a certain response. So, you don't see "cause and effect." What you see is potentiation of "likelihoods." Rain and sunshine increase the likelihood that the potentiality of growing into a flower will eventuate into an actuality. So, instead of cause and effect, what you see are conditions and likelihoods and statistical probabilities. You don't see cause and effect. "Cause and effect" is an imagination that you try to project on to something because you don't really see what's going on.

[Q]: *"Earlier you were talking about that UFOs aren't real. What is your sense about other intelligent beings that aren't on the planet Earth? Do they exist, and if they do, are they helping at all?"*

You realize there is an infinite number of universes, which are being created at an infinite rate of speed, continuously throughout all eternity. You realize that? You still want to ask the question? All we want to know is not to go there. There's an infinite number of universes expanding and being created at an infinite rate *faster* than the speed of light. Everybody thinks, "within the speed of light." No. "There's an infinite number of new universes which are created continuously at a rate faster than the speed of light-resist." [True.] The speed of light is just a human invention. Faster than the speed of light. There's an infinite number of universes.

THAT WHICH IS GOD IS PRESENT IN ALL THAT EXISTS

That which is God is present in all that exists. The Divinity that exists in all that exists itself has the essence of creativity. That which God creates has within itself the quality of Divinity, which in and of itself then manifests as the evolution of an ever-unending universe of universes. Infinite galaxies, infinite universes are expanding and coming out of Creation continuously through an infinite number of dimensions. Even from advanced theoretical physics and advanced mathematics, you realize within a one square inch cube there are an infinite number of planes. An infinite number of dimensions within one cubic inch. Therefore, in an infinite series of infinite potentialities, the likelihood that we're the only ones who can think and feel, go to the bathroom, go to Basha's, is unlikely, you know what I mean? But we will ask the question. "The answer is there's an infinite number of dimensions and an infinite number of potentialities for consciousness such as our own to grow." [True.] The answer is infinite.

Everybody likes that one. After you hear it enough times, it goes on its own within whenever you wish it to be there. And it's often very useful, because it takes you back into an energy at 740, the feelingness of like that of the great cathedral, the exquisite beauty of nature, the divinity of all creatures as created. It's more like it takes you into the memory of that reality, and that sort of pulls you out of the crisis that you're currently upset about. One just experiences the availability and the reality of that field of energy. It isn't the content of the mantra, whatever it's saying—it's the energy behind it. The essence of devotion itself. Sensitivity to exquisite beauty. The Divinity of all that exists. . . . The willingness to surrender to the love of God. . . . In the end, it will be. "And to Thee, O Lord, I surrender my life and that which I am, completely surrender it to Thee, O Lord. Amen." And that's the last thing to be answered before you walk through the final door. The willingness to surrender your life itself. Not that which you think is your life, this physicality, but the actual core of life itself. It's like we intuit where that space is. There's no book that can tell us how to get there. All the discussions we have are to clear away the obstructions. And then the light begins to, like, rise in the background, where we get the space of where All That Is takes place. And our willingness to go there is our commitment to each other as a devotional group. Our willingness to go there for ourselves and for each other. Out of our love for each other, which is not different than our love for God.

So, thank you for being here today, sharing this. God bless you all.

CHAPTER 3

The Significance of Karma

Beauty just wipes you out, and you have to avoid beauty if you're going to stay in the world. I try to avoid beauty as much as I can—and then I notice how beautiful my fingers are. It's true. That calibrates at 750. Exquisite beauty takes you beyond what the nervous system can handle. So, I said in the book I'm finishing now, that when people get to a certain level of consciousness, there's a tendency to leave the world, because one gets sort of removed by it, and you can see how hard it is to function at 750. To be in the condition that that music takes you to and take the subway and get to work on time, would be a little difficult. So, the tendency is to withdraw from the world and rebalance, if it's possible to rebalance, and to see what one's remaining capacities may be.

Today we're going to be talking about karma, a subject which is familiar to those of an Eastern background and not all that familiar to people with a Western background; however, you know, familiar to spiritual students. So, I thought I would focus today on its implications, its real significance; its complexity, and at the same time, simplicity and what it really means. We said that the entire universe is one karmic unity. There is one all-encompassing karmic totality to the Allness of all of Creation, in which everything is in, from moment to moment, incredible and in perfect balance with everything else. Harmonic perfection. Part of that perfection, harmonic perfection, is what appears to be chaotic. And that which seems to be chaotic and rule against the harmonic balance of the universe, is only so because of it being perceived in that way. That harmony includes the capacity, you might say the quantum potentiality, to suddenly become its opposite. *Bang!* Man, we were praying and singing and enjoying the incense, and all of a sudden—the bomb came out of someplace! How can that be? Doesn't that disprove the existence of God? Well, God's hard to get rid of. God just won the vote back into existence again. I was so relieved. I thought they were going to vote God out of existence, out of the money, out of the Constitution! They'd take "In God We Trust" and eliminate it. I was scared, but God made it through by three votes or something, or five votes. I remember this guy on TV trying to eliminate God from everything from our society, and I thought, Jesus, didn't he ever hear of karma?

Karma's interesting. Well, karma is really an incredibly great story. You can also skip it altogether. At any one instant, you can just completely and totally surrender all that you think you are, to God. And, of course, that could be a karmically determined event. What is the significance of karma? And in some instances, it's of profound significance. It also has the capacity to light up areas of your own life so that they make sense. Without understanding karma as is done in the West, it leaves one with really only one tool to approach God, and that's faith, because nothing in life makes sense. Why are some children born crippled and blind, born with AIDS, born from cocaine-addicted mothers with brain damage? We noted in earlier lectures that, at the moment of birth, everybody already has a calibrated level of consciousness. At the moment of birth, instantly you enter this domain at a calibrated level of consciousness.

Now, we could explain physical differences, genetically. We could say, "Well, that's genetic potpourri." The game of chance of genes and sperms and all that stuff would explain why this child is crippled, this child is blind, this child is deaf, and this child is a genius, and this child writes symphonies at age four. That would be the mechanistic, reductionistic, scientific explanation. It's just genetic chance, combinations, and permutations of all those genes and chromosomes. So, that would be fine, except when we

The Significance of Karma

calibrate their levels of consciousness, we find that the calibrated level of consciousness is completely different. That is not genetically determined. That's not determined by chromosomes. In fact, it's the other way around. Because of karmic inheritance, one automatically comes in to certain genetic and chromosomal patterns, which then become the mechanism by which that karmic propensity expresses itself.

What we see in the visible domain, the discernible domain, are consequences and not causes. The fastest spiritual advance is to jump beyond the mind's belief in causality. There is no causality anywhere in this domain. There's nothing causing anything. All is becoming that which it is out of its own karmic potentiality and fulfillment because Creation reveals itself, and as it reveals itself, perception sees it as progressive and calls it "evolution." So, from the moment of birth, there is already, let's say, a quality of karma that we can calibrate as a level of consciousness. We use this little pattern here, just sort of like a homing base, you know, so I remember where I am here in the world. Well, most of you I'm talking about aren't even on here. They didn't make it that far.

So, this domain seems to be purgatorial in its qualities. Let's ask if we've got permission to ask that. "We have permission to ask that here." [True.] "This is, um, a purgatorial-type domain–resist." [True.] "In which all opportunities exist, both high and low." [True.] "One can rise or fall." [True.] "One gets a chance to undo the negative karma." [True.] "And acquire positive karma." [True.] So, this is a formative domain, purgatorial. You can tell it's purgatorial because it goes from the very ugliest and worst and most horrific, to the most divine.

The slums of some of the poorest countries in the world where I've been, the slums are unbelievable to somebody who's grown up in the Western world, in America. To walk through those slums and see the style of life is like shocking; you don't even believe it. It's not even possible that that which calls itself "human" can survive in these conditions—eating bugs, bitten by rats, using as building materials pieces of scrap and cardboard all pasted together. They live in pieces of cardboard boxes, and maybe a

KARMA AND DEVOTION

family of 12 lives in there, and they take turns sleeping in there. Anyway, it's incredible. And everybody begs for a living. The biggest mistake is to give a begging child a penny. They're then over you like a swarm of army ants. And you realize that you're not going to be able to hold back this flood. You can hand out money to the children coming up to you, and it's not going to alter anything, because there's floods of them. As you give out handfuls of the pennies, more and more and more and more come, and more and more and more and more and more and more and more and more come. They would come from miles and miles and miles. And you see that it's not going to change anything at all, trying to change the circumstance, because what you're seeing is the effect. You're seeing the effect; you're not seeing the cause.

Certain neighborhoods pull to them that which is negative. The "broken window" theory in sociology. The first broken factory window, if you don't repair it, brings graffiti. That graffiti brings the crime. That brings the rape. That brings the robbery. That brings the drugs. That brings the arson. That brings the murder. The negative energy field then pulls to it all that which is aligned with that field.

People say, "I don't believe in karma." I don't want anybody to believe in karma, because what one is at any instant is the karmic conclusion of all that has preceded. You know, the main reason is not well understood in the West, that Jesus did not get into it to any great depth; he only mentioned it briefly as a subject. But the teachings of Christianity are that all actions have a consequence, a spiritual consequence in another domain—that it has to do with the fact that every action then has some kind of registering in the soul. Some kind of aspect of the soul registers, for all time, every action and decision. This will determine your fate in later, other dimensions. Having these hells and purgatories are pretty much accepted by all the world's religions as a reality.

Sometimes people resist karma because they have it confused with reincarnation. They are two different things. Reincarnation is one thing; karma is another. All religions teach *karma*, but they don't use that term. They don't use the terminology. Because life

The Significance of Karma

seems unfair to yourself and to others as you look around, there's a bitterness towards God, and eventually even a hatred of God comes out of the lack of understanding karma; therefore, I think it's beneficial to one's faith and understanding to understand that what you see are consequences. Consequences of things that have been brought into one's life over long expanses of time. With no understanding of karma, God then appears unfair. "How does God allow this crippled child to be born?" You hear that all the time. "Therefore, I don't believe in God."

So, failure to comprehend karma, I think, leads to a lot of atheism and agnosticism, and even eventually, rage and hatred of God because it doesn't accept responsibility. You see, with karma, you accept the responsibility that one's own decisions and prior existences are what have determined the situation. Otherwise, it looks like an arbitrary God just didn't give a rap about this kid and favored this one or what. How do you explain God?

One of the best uses of kinesiology is as a research tool. Within three minutes flat, you can satisfy all your questions about karma . . . that's if you're slow. Within about one minute flat, you can discover the likelihoods of why your life is the way it is and certain things have recurred. And as people get into spiritual study, they begin to sort of intuitively get: "You know, I must have done something in some lifetime to explain why this is the fourteenth time a white truck has run into the back of my car." Fourteen times, fourteen different cities, there's gotta be something there." You know, we've all had things, recurrent patterns in our life that are beyond explanation, that you can consult all the wise ones of the world, and frankly, they don't know 'em, they don't know the answer unless you're aware of the reality of the spiritual domain, and that it overrules the physical.

It's only when you identify a certain pattern, and then you say, "You know, it's very likely that such and such happened." And you'll find, yes, it did, in fact; such and such happened. So, all this sequence of events, and it happened, let's say, in relationships, "I must have been an SOB in some lifetime." That's the only explanation, isn't it? Why should everybody beat up on you and give

KARMA AND DEVOTION

you a hard time in your relationships in *this* lifetime? Well, they're waitin' for you, folks. "That's generally the truth of it-resist." [True.] So, you don't have to be a rocket scientist to get what it's all about, that it seems rather obvious that every decision, then, sets up a vibrational pattern somewhere in the soul body which exists over time, and thus we see in this lifetime, the externalization, the physicality, the expression of that which we have become.

I always thought that Jesus Christ didn't talk too much about karma for a couple of reasons. First of all, it would have made him unpopular in the society in which he was living. It wasn't in India, you know. It wasn't the Far East, where it would have been, "So what?" Because such things were known for a thousand years before the birth of Christ in the Far East. But where he grew up, they were pretty rudimentary. The calibrated level of consciousness at the time of Jesus was 100. At the time of the birth of Buddha, it was 90. Five hundred years later at the time of the birth of Christ, it was 100. So, he's talking to people with a consciousness level of 100, you know. And his teachings were unpopular at the time, to put it mildly. He was not exactly the popular teacher around town and to the powers that be. So, I always thought, in the height of wisdom, he just didn't bring it up as a specific topic, per se. He said it, that all your actions will have consequences in a later life. He did mention once, in Matthew, in the Bible, something about "Isaiah has come back to us as John the Baptist." In Matthew, that's the only quote making a direct reference.

On such an advanced level of consciousness, it's obvious that what you are—that the ego and your karma and that which you are—are all one and the same thing. You don't have to worry about karma; just work on what your problems are in the present, because they *are* the consequence of karma. So, you don't have to really study and teach karma. So, I thought he just bypassed it as unnecessary. He gave the folks enough to think about, anyway. A more sophisticated group . . . I think if he was speaking to people of a more advanced consciousness, there might have been greater explanation.

The Significance of Karma

As we've said in previous lectures, the purpose of the life of Jesus Christ was salvation. That he did come down directly from heaven, as a manifestation directly from heaven, and had no prior lifetimes, no human lifetimes. "That's correct-resist." [True.] So, he wasn't really gung ho on the subject to begin with, having not had a lot of previous lifetimes. His familiarities were with heaven and the nature of heaven and how one gets there and how one avoids the other direction. The Buddha, on the other hand, had many, many previous lifetimes, and therefore spoke freely of it. Let's see. "The Buddha did indeed have many previous human lifetimes-resist." [True.]

So, two different ways of approaching the subject. If what your spiritual difficulties are now is the result of your karmic inheritance from prior lifetimes, it doesn't really change it. What it does do is make it more acceptable. If buses keep running into the back of your car, and then you find in some lifetime you drove your oxen over your neighbor's gardens periodically out of paranoia, or whatever, it would make sense, huh? So, a little karmic research into your own particular grievances gets rid of self-pity. Gets rid of self-pity, indignant rage, resentment, "How could God be so unfair?" When I was a kid, everybody was going out for football. Football? Christ, I weighed 62 pounds! So, I used to hang like this every day—I thought I could stretch myself out and get taller. And I ate a lot, but I couldn't get fatter or taller, so. . . . You see, it's like unfair, isn't it? I mean, the other kids are mesomorphs; they get out there and knock the people over and wrestle with each other and all kinds of wild things . . . and I'm reading a book. Karmic propensity.

So, many people then have many resentments about many things in their life, and if you check back on them, you'll see that they were earned. They were earned, deserved, and now you're thankful for them. Because you say, well, if I was an SOB in past lifetimes, and cruel and selfish and beat my wife every day, like they do in other parts of the world . . . It's your duty to beat your wife every day in certain parts of the world. Maybe they have to come back and get beaten because they failed to beat their wife every day.

So, it puts it into proportion. Some understanding of karma, then, gets you out of self-pity, resentment, hatred, hatred of God, cursing God for being unfair, and putting you here with whatever limitations you have. And everyone has limitations.

Because all of Creation is one karmic unity, then, we represent not only personal karma, but we represent the karmic pattern, the evolution of consciousness on this planet, and to where it is evolved in the evolution of mankind. So, we're stuck with the karma of mankind itself. *Homo sapienism*, which can give you everything—arthritis, blindness, deafness, convulsions. A lot goes with it, huh? I mean, to work for a living and all those unfairnesses. It's okay to talk about the daisies in the field, neither do they labor or toil; if it wasn't for a human being out there in the field, it wouldn't be just sittin' there looking beautiful and waving in the wind! Get a shovel, daisy, and let's see how.... Fred was over at our house for the weekend and was shoveling dirt, you see. If he was a daisy, he wouldn't have to shovel dirt; he could just sit there and look pretty. He helped us out with a greenhouse which had fallen down. Its karmic propensity was to decay over time with dry rot.

CONSCIOUSNESS AND LIFE ARE ONE AND THE SAME

Understanding your karma is important to look at. That you didn't just arise spontaneously out of nowhere as you are at this moment. Now life and consciousness are one and the same. We went back into prior the universe this morning, Susan and I. I said let's go back prior. Out of the Unmanifest comes the manifest. But consciousness and life are one and the same. And they don't appear until existence, until the manifest expresses itself as existence. "That which has no existence is beyond consciousness-resist." [True.] "Out of the Unmanifest arises the manifest-resist." "The manifest is devoid of life or consciousness-resist." [True.] "Out of the manifest arises existence-resist." [True.] "Innate to existence is

The Significance of Karma

consciousness." [True.] "And consciousness and life are one and the same-resist." [True.]

"Life cannot be extinguished-resist." [True.] "Consciousness cannot be extinguished-resist." [True.] Wow. What does that mean? That means death is impossible. That which has life has life eternally, that which is conscious. You can swat the fly, but you can't kill its life energy because it flits around in the astral and comes right back as another fly. You can't extinguish life or its consciousness.

When I was a kid, it was okay to have mercury. My father would bring home mercury, which they took out of filling stations or something. And we had a wonderful collection of mercury. Now it would be illegal, I guess, because mercury vapor poisoning would send everybody into paranoid fits, and you'd have the EPA knocking at your door. But in those days, we lived in a simpler world of ignorance. We would put it in a bowl, and to amuse me, my father would pour some mercury in this thing, and I'd of course try to pick it up. I was maybe four at the time. I'd try and pick up the mercury, and it would just go that way. You pick up that one, it would go that way. No matter what you did, you can't pick up the mercury; it just moves around someplace else. Which is the way life then is—cannot be extinguished.

So, we have to give up fearing death because it's not going to be an escape hatch. No, you're not going to get out of the deal with death. Everybody grieves death: "Oh, I fear death." Come on, I know; on the other side of your consciousness, it's your big cop-out: "Oh, I'll die and get away from it all." Boy, it should be that easy, huh? No, it seems the karmic propensities then prevail, in and out, weaving through—it could be an infinite number of lifetimes. It can be an infinite number of human lifetimes. I never asked that before. "It's possible to have an infinite number of human lifetimes-resist." [True.] So! Isn't that neat? I mean, you never want to go to heaven, and you never want to go to hell; you just want to go to work every day. Propagate and have sex, eat up a storm—you can keep doing it! Wow! What a relief! Oh, mint chocolate chip ice cream, I do not have to leave thee! I get old, totter over, come back as another little kid, and have my chocolate chip mint ice cream again—no end. Endless.

You never have to return to God. Is that a fact? "You never have to return to God-resist." [True.] You never have to become enlightened-resist." [True.] "You can just keep going like this forever." [True.]

So, to some people that's going to be a relief. Other people, it means, unless you do some kind of progressive spiritual work, you're going to keep reincarnating as . . . into the physical, as a human being. "That's so-resist." [True.] "You have a choice to reincarnate-resist." [True.] "From the astral domains-resist." [True.] "So being here is a choice." [True.] "A choice, because it's a place to evolve-resist." [True.] "We have permission to ask about what I'm thinking about-resist." [True.] "The domains where people go who refuse God-resist." [True.] So, you don't have to go to God, in a number of ways. It's not necessary. You can just keep recycling. You can keep recycling until an inspiration comes to move on ahead.

And the Buddha apparently didn't like physical reincarnations because he didn't speak too highly of it. He said unless you become enlightened, you're going to have to get re-physicalized periodically or reincarnate. And of course, he was looking at the downside of human life. He was looking at old age, sorrow, poverty, and death—that those things he thought were inevitable. And that the way beyond it was to transcend karma by becoming enlightened, meaning to transcend one's identification with the ego—its origin, its function, and its structure. And to realize the Self, to realize one's Buddha nature.

Christianity does not emphasize enlightenment at all. There is in Catholicism a condition that signifies a high level of consciousness. As a lifestyle, Christianity recognizes sainthood and generally is talking about the 500s, high 500s. Like Father Pio at 590, the pope at 570. The pope, Pope John Paul II, to me is saint-like. That's just my perception; I can tell by the way he walks. He's gotten higher as he got older. You slow down as the level of consciousness grows up. You have to forcibly stay out of that certain level of consciousness, or it's not possible to function very well. So, I see he sort of fights with it.

Therefore, whatever goes on in our life currently is really the consequence of the totality of all that has gone before, as it is expressing itself under current conditions. It's not *causing* the current conditions; it's expressing itself in this way. It has the potentiality to express itself, and under these conditions that potentiality will express itself this way; and under these conditions, that potentiality will express itself this way. So, nothing is a rigid causality, an inflexible causality; on the contrary, closer to Truth is the whole concept of quantum potentiality, in which the prior orders gone before are influencing not just specifically the content of consciousness, they're influencing the whole context. So, the whole context, then, is what increases the likelihood of certain potentialities of coming into expression.

In spiritual work we, in the beginning, focus on content of consciousness: How could I have been so mean to my stepmother? How could I have been so "this and that" to my mother-in-law? And you feel guilty about how selfish you were and stole your sister's cookie, the last cookie on her birthday. You feel guilty about that for 45 years. Isn't that true? Some little dinky thing way back there, and somehow you can't get it out of your head. You took the last cookie on your sister's birthday. Oh, that selfishness, that greediness, that horribleness! You hate yourself for it. It's horrible! Fifty years later, you're still at it. Probably on death's door, you're going to say, "God, I stole my sister's cookie, please, let me off the hook." Guilt just looks for something to anchor itself into. It isn't just the guilt about your sister's cookie; it's all the accumulated guilt about everything throughout all of lifetimes anchoring itself into this particular expression.

Some comprehension of the nature of karma and maybe how it came about in your own lifetime can facilitate certain difficult things to transcend, make them easier. Make them easier to transcend; and I'm sure some things from other lifetimes with it, you know, and have sort of fun with it. We can have fun with it, because now in this lifetime I can look back, and now I can feel light about it. I'm sure at the time, I didn't feel all that light about it. It's because we recontextualize it.

Sometimes if you're stuck in something, you can ask, "is this is karmic propensity?" Was it that? Usually what you look for is the opposite; you look for the opposite. What's happening to you, you ask, "Was that what I did to others in my past life and now I see what it's like?" So, one of the ways the mind undoes its guilt is to undo it by living it through and living the side of the victim. So, in the prior lifetime where you were the perpetrator, you now have the responsibility in this lifetime to undo that, either by good works or by experiencing it out and forgiving everything and everyone, including yourself. So, the tool that helps you through all of this is, first of all, the comprehension does make many things easier to accept, that if you can go back with kinesiology and say, "In some lifetime did I do such-and-such, or did such-and-such a thing happen?" Then you can get sort of an "Aha! I guess it makes sense then."

Early in life I'd never heard of karma, but I would always say, "I must have done something to somebody in some lifetime to deserve that," you know what I'm saying? It just sort of made sense; otherwise, there would be no other explanation for it, except that God is arbitrary and a sadist.

There are many atheists in the world, and they're not all stupid; many of them are quite brilliant. When they look at the world through the Newtonian paradigm of reality, the idea that there's an infinite, benevolent God who is not different than Love is idiotic. Understand? Logic, reason, at a certain point will not take you to God; it will take you to atheism. At one level of consciousness, if you're not an atheist, I think you're stupid. I was a devout atheist for years, and I looked at anybody who believed in God as an absolute idiot. You look at the disaster of mankind and say, "God is the Source of all this? Well, you can keep Him." So, that was when I held God as the Source—the *cause* of the human karmic dilemma.

What we see, then, as human tragedy is the effect of the ego, uncaused by God. So, it's as though the capacity for existence and

The Significance of Karma

life and consciousness is a given. And then what is done with it becomes one's own karmic responsibility, the consequences of which we see collectively as society. But, when I became an atheist, it was because the totality of the suffering of all of mankind opened up as a revelation. It was staggering. I was a devout religionist at the time and scrupulous, in fact, scrupulous. I told you how I used to dread Saturday afternoon when you went to confession so that you wouldn't sin someplace before you went to church on Sunday morning and have communion. Anyway, I was out in the woods, and suddenly the totality of the suffering of all of mankind throughout all of time opened up in the most staggering revelation, beyond the capacity of ordinary human thinkingness to comprehend. In that instant I became an atheist. *Bam*—God went out that fast. I can't believe in a God that allows that. Because, when you look at the totality of human suffering, one has to be of a sizable dimension to even glance at it. It just blows you away. In clinical practice, you know, you see it piecemeal. You see it piecemeal in the ER. In war you see it piecemeal. But this came on, not piecemeal, but *all* of it. Whoo! Was I ever a devout atheist, and I took Catholicism apart, Protestantism apart, the Reformation apart, the Bible—idiotic! Thomas Aquinas. Good God, give me a break! I got straight A in Theology in a Jesuit university. Straight A in Ethics, straight A in Logic, straight A in Theology. Because if you're going to be against something, you better know a lot about it. So, Friday afternoon outside of Marquette University, in Louie's bar—we had all our names on our mugs—I sat in the corner and I took on all comers. All the religionists. And I would knock 'em out of the box, one after another. Never lost a round; that's a fact. Never lost a round.

Because within the Newtonian paradigm of reality, nothing about God is really provable; you have to go to the nonlinear, where you're beyond causality, you're beyond logic, you're beyond literalism and concrete, and you get to greater dimensions. So, it takes the greater dimensions to heal the negativities that have arisen out of karma. Now, whatever one has inherited in one way or another, or come into, because you come into it just by being human, you share in human consciousness. The totality of human consciousness is something which dominates individual consciousness.

The reason you can light up a whole crowd of enthusiasts about something is because that consciousness level is available to the whole crowd. Adolph Hitler knew how to play that; like he would play 10,000 people shouting, *"Sieg Heil"* at the same time, and it was hypnotic, you know. If you weren't a Nazi in those years of Germany, you must have been brain dead, because it was persuasive; it was all-encompassing; it was powerful; it was patriotic; it was military; it was grand. The fact that it was somewhat in error did not show up until later, but at the time, it was.... You know, any normal kid would want to go to one of the boy's camps and learn how to become a member of the Hitler youth. There'd have to be something wrong with you not to want to, because it was so prevailing in society.

So, we see how these dominant levels of consciousness have resonated in the human condition, because everybody in that crowd is a captive of the human condition. They're all born with the capacity for loyalty, nationalism, enthusiasm, macho masculinity, militarism, all those things. You inherit that as part of being a human.

About the worst thing you see go on in the world historically, currently, it is really the consequence of being human. To be a human being . . . to begin with, a human being can't tell truth from falsehood. A walking, stumbling idiot. How did we ever get this far? I don't know.

It boggles me that we even got here. Can you imagine a species that doesn't know truth from falsehood? If you don't know truth from falsehood, that pretty much puts you back in the animal kingdom, where you're instinctual, stimulus and response. Of course, this became more elaborate in the hominid, became more elaborate in Neanderthal man, *Homo erectus*. It became more elaborate, but still its innate nature didn't change at all—greed, fear, attack, counterattack. Anything you see in Monkey Island is in every day's newspaper. No different at all. There's no difference between human society and Monkey Island. Little groups ganging up on each other, little gossipers like this, people getting some quick sex on the side while the people aren't looking. People running in to grab things. Someone was telling me about how he was watching how life is. The monkey grabs something, and a bigger monkey comes along and takes it away from him. Then a bigger monkey comes and knocks him out and takes it away from him. Then the big monkey comes along, hits him over the head, and takes the whole deal. So, that's today's political news, isn't it?

So, the political position that we're going to take now, is to stand up! Take us on and you've got big trouble! The best defense is a good offense, huh? Well, it's been tried all different ways; we'll see how it works this time. I saw how it worked in World War II—pacificism and peace are not the same thing. So, we'll take a stand and look fierce and see if that holds off anybody with any common sense, but megalomaniacs don't have common sense. You say, "Walk across the line and we'll shoot you." They'll still walk across the line because there's some nuts and bolts missing. "Nobody will do anything so stupid," is what we rely on. We've been wrong over and over again. Nobody would be so stupid as to so-and-so. Oh, yeah, they would. They would.

So, we have the karmic unity of the universe. Then, Creation expressing itself through consciousness and the energy of life, evolving up through the animal kingdom, we see consciousness becoming more and more conscious, more and more subtle, more advanced: the progression of Consciousness up to the point of *Homo sapiens*. Then we see *Homo sapiens* calibrated at 90 at the time of Buddha; a 100 at the time of Jesus; 190 throughout the centuries.

The 1700s. Let's just do it, because I don't know if we ever did it here. "The consciousness level of mankind in the 1700s—we have permission to ask that in here." [True.] "Was over 185." [Not true.] No, 185. "In the 1900s—in the early 1900s, it was over 185." [True.] "188." [Not true.] "In 1900, the consciousness level of mankind was over 188." [True.] "189." [Not true.] 189, okay. "In the 1950s, the consciousness level of mankind was over 190." [True.]

"191." [Not true.] It was still 190. "In 1980, the consciousness level was over 190-resist." [True.] "192." [Not true.] 190. "In 1986, the consciousness level of mankind was over 190-resist." [True.] "191." [True.] "193." [True.] "195." [Not true.] 1986. "In 1988, the consciousness level was over 200-resist." [True.] "205." [True.] "206." [Not true.]

Wow, right there in the late '80s, suddenly all of the potentiality for human life totally changed, of a greater significance than the temperature of the earth going up two degrees. To go from, let's see, 190 in my own lifetime, then, the consciousness level went up, let's see. "When I was born, the consciousness level of mankind was over 180." [True.] "182." [True.] "184." [Not true.] 184. When I was born, it was 184. Now, it's 207. Um, that's a very, very major change. Very major change.

It means that karmically, you might say, the entire human race has evolved. You see, we're carried along by the wave of the advance of consciousness of *all* of mankind. The karmic potentiality of humanness itself, as well as one's own individual karma. One also shares sort of an ethnic karma, national karma. If you live in a certain country, you sort of share the fate of that whole country, don't you? When it goes down, you go down with it. So, we have an infinite number of components to what one would call one's own individual karma. It's not individual, but we call it individual because it's unique in certain patterns peculiar to your own prior lifetimes. Let's just reaffirm that with kinesiology. "What I just said is a fact-resist." [True.] Okay. Most people in this room have lived many previous physical lifetimes-resist." [True.] "The average is even more than eight." [True.] "12." [True.] "20." [True.] "25." [Not true.] "The average of lifetimes of everybody in this room is about 24." [True.] "25." [True.] "26." [Not true.] So, that's just of academic interest.

So, if all of us have lived an average of 24 lifetimes, some people are greedy and lived 50 or 60, you know; there are others have had only 4 or 5. Some people are smart and only had one previous lifetime, and that's going to be their last, you know what I mean? "I got it the last time." The importance of it is you have got it now.

The importance is that we have it now. However, what we're trying to do is recontextualize it so that way you don't take it so personally, so you don't feel bad about it, because I don't like to encourage people into spiritual introspection unless the capacities to be hard on yourself are alleviated.

THE WORLD IS A PROJECTION OF THE EGO

In psychoanalysis, the first rule is to approach the patient from the side of the superego. First, relieve their excessive punitive conscience before you start digging up material from the unconscious. First, get the conscience to be a little bit more reasonable before you start looking at ulterior motives and things that are repressed. The reason they're repressed is because they're so hateful, because they make you feel so guilty, because they're so awful that you wouldn't tell anybody on the planet. Now, you're supposed to lie on the couch and reveal them to your analyst. The analyst aligns himself with the person's healthy side and tries to ameliorate the sadistic nature of the superego. The conscience tends to be sadistic. You see that expressed in society. We don't want to just capture the bad people, we want to kill 'em, exterminate 'em, electrocute 'em, and torture 'em a little bit before they go. Yes, that's what your superego has in store for you.

That which you have condemned others to is *exactly* what your unconscious condemns you to. You cannot judge savagely *out there* and think that when it comes up within yourself, because the superego will not differentiate between you and others. Stealing a cookie requires death. That's the kind of superego I used to have—I mean, I know it.

So, we want to ameliorate our view of the world and our relationship with the world because the world is a projection of the ego. The savagery that you hold against the world is nothing but a mirror that you hold against yourself. Now, you must have very severe things that you're holding against yourself; otherwise, everyone would become enlightened. You realize that the Self, the Source of that which is listening right now is God. Everybody just became enlightened. Some of you didn't accept it. No? Why not? Maybe we should try it the other way. Anyone who doesn't completely and totally surrender to God right now, we shall electrocute! Oh, I saw them let go of another one!

So, spiritual work is becoming acquainted with the subtleties. You become aware of it subtly. Now the question is, how to approach it. How to undo that propensity without going into excessive guilt about it. You can't go into squirming, hair shirt self-torture over every indelicate comment you might have made offhand. After a while you see that it's an indulgence. Excessive guilt is just another indulgence. It's another addiction, it's another spiritual error to. . . . So, one has to surrender one's sense of guilt and self-punitive quality to God. The willingness to surrender self-punitive, self-hatred, guilt, and shame.

The next block that comes up when you try to do that is that there's a belief system, especially arising out of Christianity, that the only propitiation for sin is suffering. You'll find that the real Christian is really addicted to suffering. And the way to God is through suffering, penance, crawling through the streets of the city over the cobblestones with the blood running out of your knees, not eating, not taking a bath, crawling from here to some holy place. Penance, suffering, pain, then, are addictions; they are excesses. They are indulgences that one has to be willing to surrender to God.

That which is the Infinite Source of all of Creation is not impressed by bleeding knees, self-flagellation, burning off your fingers and toes, chopping off your thumb, other insanities. Spiritual insanity. The totality of all of Creation, then, shines forth as one's existence at this moment, and, as a result of karmic propensities, one is at this particular point in some kind of a purgatorial realm where the opportunity to transcend all that is present at all times. In a true purgatory, then, you get to undo the negatives of the past and choose the positive—you get a chance to "undo." We've got ministers here who are authorities on purgatory; I'm not an authority on purgatory. It just has always seemed to me that in a domain where you can go from the most horrid to the

The Significance of Karma

most exquisite, that that is really the nature of purgatory. Limbo is where you just hang out and wait to go one place or another; I'm trying to remember Catholic theology. Limbo is where you sort of hang out; you don't go one place or another; you're sort of marking time or something. Purgatory, you get a chance to undo your errors and earn your way into higher dimensions. The heavens are then the consequence of having undone the required amount of negative karma, that one's consciousness level is now consistent with more heavenly domains.

We get from research that consciousness—that we need a savior below levels of 600. Let's see. "Entities who leave the body at less than 600 require the intervention of a savior to enter heaven-resist." [True.] Yes. So, a savior, a guru, a higher teaching is necessary. The ancient wisdom is that without the assistance of higher Truth, from whatever its source, the likelihood is that unaided, the individual lacks sufficient spiritual power to overcome the ego. That makes the ego sound quite formidable, doesn't it?

"So, just spiritual truth, such as knowledge, in itself has the intrinsic action of the guru—the truth itself-resist." [True.] Okay. "To merely hear the truth already has the effect of the blessing of the guru-resist." [True.] Okay, okay. So, to merely hear, to merely know certain things, is already elevating, already advances one's consciousness, has a catalytic effect. Sometimes, just one little piece of information, like *whoosh!*—solves all kinds of little things in the puzzle. They all make sense. Sometimes, karmic research does that. Karmic research back, and you'll find some single event or collection of events are propensities of certain lifetimes. And now you see that, over and over again, you're asked to transcend that. To value money over life. "In the lifetime I'm thinking of, I valued money over life-resist." [True.] "Greed over life." [True.] Yeah. To let people die out of greed. To value gain, greed, money, treasure over the value of human life, to sacrifice human life for money, umm, yeah.

That's a pretty common one, right? Anybody that's lived before is likely to have done that, right? Why? Because human consciousness has evolved up through the animal kingdom. Unless you're a greedy animal, you really don't survive. How long does an altruistic animal survive? "Here, Hubert, you can have my bone. And, if there's any left, I will have what's left." "Grrrrr, sorry hon." Well, you get smaller and smaller, and finally you fall over. So, our first commitment is to be a good animal. You have to have a certain gusto for life and a certain love of life and enthusiasm for life. You've got to have the capacity to get in there and *whap!* There are times when you've got to do that—it's the only spiritual thing you can do. Feeble monks aren't worth a nickel. "I'm praying." "Get off your knees, old man, and sweep the floor! Don't you see all the crap around here!"

Well, one of my secret ambitions I have to let it go, is to be a verger in a great cathedral. Can you imagine? You know, here's a janitor—you don't have to talk to anybody, say anything to anybody. People are idiotic; you have to listen to their prattle. You get to hear the choir practicing Thursday nights, Wednesday nights. You get to live around incense, stained glass windows, incredible sculpture, incredible beauty. It's a way to God. I think God is jealous of the. . . . He keeps the job of janitor in the great cathedral for his favorite ones. If I'm to have another lifetime, I'd like to be a verger in a great—nah, cancel that one. Because, by then, they'll have all kinds of regulations. Fingerprint, register, and—you know what I mean?—verger regs coming out from the Welfare Department. The day of the verger in the great cathedral is over. Let's see. "That's an attachment to a previous lifetime." [True.] Aha. So, the minute I hear that music, it throws me into the Ecstasy of beauty, you know, which is a very rapid pathway to God. Because to just immerse oneself in beauty, the oneness of beauty and God and the Self, suddenly the barriers dissolve. One is all of that.

Just as aversions come from past lifetimes, the minute I heard that music, I could feel the longing for that lifetime to be a verger. I didn't realize it was a previous lifetime; I thought it was a fantasy lifetime, to be the verger in a great cathedral; and of course, when I go to Europe, I go from cathedral to cathedral. Some people go from Berlin to Paris to London; I just go from St. Pat's to, you know, one cathedral to another. That attachment to cathedrals, to be of silent service to God in the presence of that beauty as a form of worship, is an attachment.

So, the karma then plays a part in our ambitions, our daydreams, the limitation of what we think we can be or accomplish in this lifetime. Obviously, people who are in a group like this have responded to that which within them is telling them that the pathway to spiritual evolution is theirs, so people in a room like this have already evolved to an incredibly advanced degree. We've said that only 4 percent of the world's population ever gets over the 400s. Four percent. Only 4 percent are able to transcend logic and reason. So, although this is the crown jewel—logic and reason is the alleged crown jewel of man—the difference between man and animals is that man can think. This is supposedly the crown jewel of man, from the viewpoint of education, the viewpoint of the social evolution, the capacity to think and reason, to be able to develop science and all the great benefits of science. So, the 400s are enormously beneficial. Without the 400s, half of us wouldn't be in this room; we would have died of things that we now cure with penicillin and streptomycin and surgery and many other things.

So, Reason is the great salvation from the animal world. So, down here on the Map, we are stuck in the animal world, then we transcend into humanness, and with the exception of kitties and dogs, who somehow passed us by—I don't know how they got up there—we hit Willingness. Willingness is different than ambition. Ambition will get you through medical school. You've got to be a workhorse. But to be a good doctor takes something else. It takes willingness. Then it takes something different—willingness, acceptance, and easygoing-ness, and then finally an unconditional compassion for human suffering.

But those are beyond Reason. But in a group like this, we know that because of one's karmic propensity, then, one is evolved up into the 400s. In the 400s we read, we go to lectures, we visit cathedrals, we begin to appreciate that there is already within us

KARMA AND DEVOTION

the higher levels of consciousness, and it's merely a matter of identifying with them.

So, everyone here already has the highest level of consciousness within them. And the difficulty, then, is not the failure to acknowledge it, because many people in this room are quite devout, but the habit of identifying with the mind, with the ego, with logic as who you are. So, the problem, then, is really one of identification: to identify with the content rather than the context. To identify with the content of form, logic, reason, feeling, etc., and to fail to realize that one is context.

Anybody ever seen *Mail Call*, Sunday nights on the History Channel? It's hysterical if you're a vet of World War II. But the lead actor in that, he comes on like a caricature of the top sergeant, you know. And he says, "Don't touch that channel! Nobody gave you permission! I'll tell you when it's time to leave this podium!" It just breaks me up because it represents that anything, if recontextualized, totally changes its flavor and significance, you see? In other words, in that context his attitude is hysterically funny, because you're not a victim. In another circumstance, he'd be terrifying. When I was 17 years old, the top boatswain's mate, you know, would terrify me. "Holy Christ," your heart would start beating. So, the context was different.

* * *

So, that which is God and that which is beauty are one and the same. I don't like to talk about it, the pathway of the heart, because it doesn't last long. Adoration, devotion, worship. Someone asked, "How do you get beyond the thinkingness of the mind?" And beauty is one of the most immediate ways. The beauty of the music takes you out of thinkingness in one instant. It's like incredible beauty immobilizes you. So, beauty, then, is the awareness of the Grace of God, which is different than discussing the various things we discuss. It's the way around the mind.

Somebody asked, *How do you stop that thinkingness?* You become enamored of God instead of enamored of the thoughts.

The Significance of Karma

To discern the Presence of God in all that exists is a gift that suddenly comes forth of its own with the willingness to surrender all that stands in its way. The gratification, the satisfaction, the excitement of thinkingness, feelingness, emotions. It's a great leap because we transcend the instincts of the animal. We transcend the thinkingness of *Homo sapien* and respond to the Divinity within us.

We said this morning and verified it—out of the Unmanifest arises the manifest. Out of the manifest arises existence as beingness. With that existence arises consciousness and the energy of life. Therefore, all that has life arises from the Unmanifest through the manifest, through existence and beingness, through consciousness and awareness. All that is created by God has within it, Divinity. Let's see if that's so. "All that exists has within it, its Source as Divinity-resist." [True.] Consequently, then, the awareness of the Presence of God as the Source of one's own existence is innate within consciousness itself. It is already present. And it's only a matter of letting go of the identifications with all that stand in its way.

The purposes of the lectures prior to last month were to, by familiarity and by description and by analysis, understand the structure of the ego. And, by understanding it, have the capacity to disassemble it. And we always start the lectures by reminding ourselves that All That Is, is what it is, by virtue of the Divinity of its creation. Each thing is only becoming, manifesting you might say, its karmic propensity to be that which it is. Therefore, there's no reason to worry about God, or reaching God or being with God or anything, because one is constantly in the Presence of God, who is the Source of consciousness, out of which arises your worrying about God.

There's no need to worry about God. It's only the capacity to appreciate beauty. The exquisite power of perfection. So, beauty is a style of recognizing the perfection of all that exists. As spiritual awareness progresses, the awareness of the perfection and intrinsic beauty of all that exists becomes overwhelming. And at a certain point it becomes incapacitating. And if the music is beautiful enough, you can't stand up and talk; you have to sit down now. Whether the body eats or doesn't eat—you can see how quickly all that becomes irrelevant. You go into a state of spiritual Ecstasy; the survival of the physicality depends on your neighbors. If you have friendly neighbors that drop in, the body survives. If not, it doesn't. And it's totally immaterial. Somebody says it's time to eat now, and so you eat; otherwise, you completely forget all about it.

As you get into the higher levels of the 500s, you know, you get into a benevolence towards life, a benevolence towards yourself, a benevolence to all that exists. There's a benevolence towards even the most horrific, because it cannot help itself but be what it is. It doesn't have the karmic whatever-it-takes to not be other than that which it is. And then, at a greater level one says, "There is no reason for it to be other than what it is." It can just be what it is—not particularly saintly, but so it is what it is. And there's letting go wanting to change anything as it is, because you see, the only thing you want to change is your perception of it all and your judgmentalism about it. You want bin Laden to be different than what he is. No, I don't want bin Laden to be different than what he is. Then who would be bin Laden? Somebody's got to be the bad example of the day, you know what I mean? Hitler, Mussolini . . . You hear all the bad guys when I was young. New guys arise on the stage.

And in the highest dimension, one sees that that is all, um, like a hologram. And there's no point to change the hologram because it's evolving out of its own intrinsic, innate, perfect balance and order within itself. All is merely becoming that which it is in its expression within physicality. There's no need to change *anything.* We become our potential, not because it's going to "do" something for the world, not because it's going to "do" something for us. Those are kindly thoughts. But in actuality, the overall consciousness field of mankind, elevating is developing because of who we are. The only thing you need to do to better the life of all mankind is to appreciate the beauty of that incredible music. You've done all you can do. To acknowledge the Presence of God, to feel the exquisite joy of that beauty sends out a vibration—of

The Significance of Karma

such immense power, you see, because power cannot be resisted, whereas force can. The power of your adoration of God, your love, your devotion radiates out and elevates the whole field of consciousness. And it affects millions of people, who are not even aware they are being afflicted. Just as the person is about to do "this" something he says, he lets it go. He doesn't know why he let it go. Because the field is so high now, it makes that kind of action almost impossible. So, what we do then, is, by the realization of our own innate perfection, impact the consciousness of all of mankind.

We calibrated the level of consciousness as it moved forward over the centuries. In the late 1980s, that was the time of the Harmonic Convergence. That was the time when all the spiritual committed people in the world joined together at a certain hour of the morning. We all woke up at 4 A.M. or something and prayed for peace. That was the time when monolithic, atheistic Communism collapsed. All of those things—and I suppose there was some kind of a confluence astrologically, not because the astrologic formation causes things, but because that which brings peace brings simultaneously many things all at the same time that are in concordance with each other, huh?

So, we're part of that emergence. We're the leading edge of *Homo spiritus*, the evolution of a new being—*Homo spiritus*. When the evolution of consciousness crossed over 200, it signaled the emergence of a new level of life, a new potentiality of life. Because it's a more powerful level of consciousness, then, it is of assistance to spiritual progression. So, my guess is that spiritual awareness will progress more rapidly and reach more people than it has in the past, profoundly affect more aspects of society. We see that within the last few months. We see that back when the consciousness level was below 190, when I grew up, winning, gain, wealth, prestige, fame, having a Cadillac, titles, degrees, all the gains, the worldly gains, the corner office with two windows, having three secretaries, the right address. That which was sought was "gain." Its downside was victory over one's enemy—kill the Japanese, kill the Nazis, kill somebody. Always to kill somebody—kill your enemies. So, the criteria of success were you went to war, you killed your enemies, then you came home, got a degree, got doctorates, made millions of dollars, lived in the best place. That was the signal of success—to be a millionaire. There's a TV program, *Who Wants to Be a Millionaire*. I know it sounds stupid, you know; it sounds so juvenile, but at the time it was very exciting. I remember when "The $64 Question" was exciting. Sixty-four dollars would get you from here to New York and back, you know; now, it wouldn't get you to Cottonwood. Wouldn't get you in and out of Walmart, that's for sure. I said, "By God, this time I'm going to Walmart, and I'm just going to buy those screens. That's all I'm buying, those grills." One hundred sixty-three dollars it cost me.

Well, now we see all that's changed. Now we wouldn't even know our enemies, even questioned. We're going through soul-searching. We've got some really heavy-duty enemies out there. And the whole country is examining their conscience. Is it okay to go after your enemies or not? Defend yourself against them or stand up to them or put them out of business before they do you in? So, the new yardstick of success, the new yardstick in society is integrity. Integrity is where it's at right now. Because of lack of integrity, we see the multimillionaire corporations collapse—Enron and Alltel and all those? They sought the old paradigm: success at any cost.

Back at the time of the robber barons, I mean, what was all that? I mean, there wasn't anything immoral about working the workers to death and firing them before Christmas. You know, big corporations always fired them the week before Christmas. And I'd say, "Good God, have they no sense at all? Don't they have any public relations person? They have just injured their corporation far more—they spend millions on advertising, and then they fire; they always do the big layoffs the week before Christmas. In the public esteem, they went from here down to here, you know what I mean? Couldn't they wait till the week *after* Christmas? Always the week before Christmas. I don't know, if you grew up in the '50s and '40s and '60s, they all would lay them off a week before Christmas. No, the new level to which we're answerable now is integrity.

Because of lack of integrity, Martha Stewart, multimillionaire, had to resign from the board of directors of the stock market. Not because she was convicted of anything, but because her integrity was now in question. That was never heard of years ago. All of you who are older, did you ever hear of anybody getting knocked off the board of directors of some corporation for lack of integrity? Never heard of it. He *got* his job by having lack of integrity. If you didn't have lack of integrity, you were never going to be a salesman in *that* company, I'll tell you. Tell a man, just get him to sign the dotted line, and make sure the check gets certified; that's the rule. When I was a salesman, you were supposed to accompany the customer to the bank.

CHAPTER 4

A New Paradigm of Reality

So, we have a new paradigm of reality now. A very powerful paradigm. Even the networks, which their integrity was questionable at times, are counting integrity as the new paradigm of reality. Not success. Nobody gives a rap about your success. Being a millionaire doesn't mean anything. All kinds of poor folks became millionaires during the high-tech stock market expansion. I had patients who could hardly afford a tank of gas, but they were millionaires. Every day they'd check their stocks on their computer, you know. God, they're worth $10 million, you know. By noon, they're worth $12 million. By three in the afternoon, they're worth $14 million—except they lack integrity, see. So now, "I want to be a millionaire" sounds sort of stupid. Everybody got a chance to shop to be a millionaire. If you didn't, your aunt did, or your neighbor did. I mean, being a millionaire doesn't mean anything. Success doesn't mean anything.

What holds up long term is integrity, and everybody knows that. The business we calibrated before we published *Power vs. Force* as integrous is now the biggest corporation in the world. If that doesn't prove that integrity pays, then what does? So, business now, some members of this group here are working to carry that message into business, that your bottom line nowadays doesn't depend on how many you sell. That'll give you a little pop on your stock, but it's not going to carry you through. I wouldn't put that in your 401(k), folks. What you'd better put in your 401(k) is

KARMA AND DEVOTION

integrity, so that 30 years from now when you need that 401(k), it hasn't gone down the drain. The only thing I know that will keep it from going down the drain is integrity. Why? Because integrity itself, just like the broken window drags that which is negative to it, that which is positive pulls that which is positive to it. I'd like to be a greeter in Walmart. I'd really like that as a job. I mean, I'd just love it—you just hug people all day and love 'em. "What can I do for you?" "Where's the underwear?" "Where's the hats?" I mean, what a fun job, you know. Almost as fun as being a cab driver. I liked being a cab driver. Oh, that was fun. Be a cab driver, you chatter, and you are friends with all the people; by the time they leave the cab, you're best buddies, you know what I mean? He wants your phone number—he wants you to come to his sister's birthday party next week. The chance to just love lots of people unconditionally is just, you know, a really great opportunity. It's probably why I gave up being a verger in a cathedral.

The life of the solitary monk has its virtue. Everybody needs a life as a solitary monk. It's a great life, because through that absolute aloneness, the simplicity—to just have a candle and a stick and a book and a chair, you really don't need anything more. You really do not need anything more. When I came out to Sedona, that's how I lived here for quite a while, with a box and a candle, with an apple, and a cot from the dime store. It was fantastic. Then life got worse—I started to own things! Got worse and worse! You become a captive of your own possessions. You become their slave, their servant.

So, we find God through simplicity, through renunciation. The renunciation can be physical, social. The renunciation is internal; to renounce, to be willing to surrender out of devotion to God the satisfaction and the gratification one gets out of one's mental gyrations—to juice revenge, to juice resentment, to juice self-pity; at the same time, not make them wrong. You see, we let go of these positions, we let go of our attachments to them, but not out of guilt and making them wrong. I like to complain and grumble. I say to her, "Honey, if we didn't have each other to complain and grumble to, who the heck would we talk to?" Now, one of our forms of love is we both listen to each other's grumbles. "The air conditioner on my car doesn't work now. And I can't drive it to Phoenix now because it doesn't work." She says, "Oh, that's awful; you can take my car." A close neighbor who works with us, Lou, has computer trouble with his car. I hope he complains to somebody. He hasn't complained to me, but if I were him, I would complain about it. "I paid good money for that car, and my computer doesn't work." You've got to have somebody to grumble to and be human with.

So, you see, you take your own self with a dash of salt, you know what I mean? You can't take yourself too seriously. You can indulge yourself, but not take it too seriously. You can have a tantrum; you can throw yourself on the floor. It's good. It's good; it's fun; you just throw yourself on the floor, and you scream with anger and hit the floor. Within everybody is a six-month-old. So, you don't make it wrong, see what I mean? Within all of us is the vindictive judge. "You're going to be put away and suffer for this, young man! And never see the light of day!" He'd say, "Yes, sir."

To transcend something, you have to be able to accept it. To accept it, you have to get off "right and wrong" about it. It just *is* that way. There are ugly little creatures in the sea. Their mothers love them, but nobody else does. It's all right for them to be there because consciousness evolves, and it expresses itself in form throughout its evolution. So, if we look around the manifest world, we see all these levels of consciousness, some lower than what we even have on the chart—poisonous little things that live at the bottom of the sea. So, it's like all these levels of consciousness express themself in form. Each one, then, is like a stepping stone. We look within ourselves, and we see all that's possible within the field of consciousness. All the positives and all of the things we call "negatives" and all. We get off our positionality about our own positionalities. It's natural to have positionalities—"right and wrong," "good and evil," "love and hate." They are not opposites; they're positionalities. They're all positionalities along the same line—they're not opposites. So, we have to always confirm that, because to undo the ego, you have to let go positionalities,

KARMA AND DEVOTION

and positionalities are set up by the dualistic thinkingness of the mind. And mind tends to think in dualistic thinking. In one instant, you'll get what it takes 50 years of meditation to "get." This will save you all kinds of "monk times." And the lousy food that goes with being a monk. You hang out in the wrong monastery where humility takes a dietary form. Porridge and turnips, that's all you get there. Not many clothes to wear. Forget turning on the heat in the wintertime. Austerity and renunciation, and then you become a rack of bones.

As we said, there's no such thing as polarities. What we see here is the presence of heat. And as the presence of heat diminishes, now we call it something different—we call it "cold" and we call this "zero." But you can see that's arbitrary. There's only one variable—the presence of heat or its absence, that's all. There's the presence of love or its absence. We become friendly, the first form that forgiveness, becoming benign, benevolent, forgiving, generous, compassionate, accepting, affectionate, is towards yourself. We practice it by looking out into the world and seeing what it is "out there" that we're still judgmental about, can't accept, can't forgive, etc., because that's within yourself, projected out into the world. The world serves, it serves us, spiritually, that the structure of society and operation are the ego projected "out there" for us to understand.

So, that way, the world serves us. It's a constant source of teaching, of learning, of opportunity. The capacity to witness because it's "out there"; it's easier to accept. We can see the cruelty out there because it's "out there" and it's "them." Because of guilt we don't see it within ourselves. We become more sensitive to it. And then, what we do is, because we're spiritually committed, is we let it go within ourselves, and in so doing, we serve the world. Everything that we let go within ourselves, we let go also within the world. The field of consciousness itself is affecting everyone. So, let's see if that's so. "Everything I serve within myself therefore serves the world-resist." [True.] Everything you let go within yourself, you're thereby serving the world. Why? Because you are part

A New Paradigm of Reality

of the world; you can't forgive it in yourself and not have the world benefit, because you *are* the world. You are one with the world.

Therefore, all the spiritual work we do within ourselves, we can consciously dedicate it to God, consciously dedicate it to our fellow human beings. It's better than, better than parades. Parades don't really change anything. "Down with whatever!" You know what I mean? That's okay for adolescents, part of college life—you get out there and get in a parade, a protest parade about something.

So, we end up loving all of life in all of its expressions without judgmentalism, and in so doing, we accept it within ourselves and vice versa. That which we accept within ourselves, we see that there's nothing we need to do.

If this is an exercise gym, if this is purgatorial, then why would you want to eliminate all the possibilities to express all the aspects of consciousness "out there"? If they can't beat up little babies here in this neighborhood, they're going to find some other little neighborhood to beat up little babies, because the horrific is part of nature, the horrific. There's no point, then, to try to change what's "out there," because the world as we see it, then, is a projection from our own ego.

So, we heal it within ourselves, and in healing within ourselves, we heal it within the world. That must be so, because we see that consciousness is progressing. It's poised at 207—207 is very profound. Integrity is stunningly, enormously important. It is the whole crux; it's the fulcrum upon which the balance tips one way or the other, is integrity. That calibrates at 200. So, we see the importance of the scale of consciousness. What is the importance of the scale of consciousness? It's that it just makes visible that which seems to be less real if it's only verbalized. We only verbalize it, see. But, if we also put it in sort of a visible form, this is the way the mind is used to thinking. We've been trained this way from kindergarten on up, to think logically, to put things in form and concept, comprehensible. So, the 400s are very useful because they're the great springboard on up to the higher levels.

We see that there's one chart that has the 200-line demarcated with some kind of color or something, to emphasize its

KARMA AND DEVOTION

importance. This one's really a better visual because it points out, it emphasizes the *importance* of this level here. This is the most crucial level on the whole map, because from here, once you cross this line, the rest is practically guaranteed, the rest is accessible. The more one rises, the more one is likely to rise. Let's see if that's so. "The higher one gets, the more likely one is to get ever higher-resist." [True.] Okay, so, the more you advance, the more you're likely to advance, and the more you advance from wanting to advance, the more advanced you get to be more advanced. So, it's an upward spiral.

Once you begin to become interested in spiritual matters, once you have the slightest interest in spirituality, then you're already on your way. Therefore, there's no worry, no need to worry, because nobody would be at a meeting like this unless they were scheduled for enlightenment, any more than you would be at divers' lessons unless you were planning to go deep-sea diving.

So, we can say then, the way is certain for all of those. The Buddha said that: "Once you've heard of enlightenment, you'll never be satisfied with anything less." To merely have heard it, already imprints consciousness. To be in the presence of those who have gone the route already impresses a vibration within consciousness. Nothing less will suffice, evermore. And so, the end is certain. So, we can stop worrying about it. Don't worry about it. You don't have to worry about it. See, because we're not just propelled from that which has occurred in the past; we are attracted by that which is destined in the future. It's only within the Newtonian paradigm that one sees present things as being caused by the past. In the quantum reality, the future is just as powerful as the past. One is not greater than the other. The pull of the future is as great or greater than the drag of the past. We'll put it in common language. "We have permission to ask that-resist." [True.] "That is a fact-resist." [True.] Don't worry about your past. "Everybody here has a fantastic future-resist." [True.] Of course.

You're not here out of guilt out of the past. You're here out of the joy that's pulling you to the future. You're like magnetically attracted to Truth, Love, that which is benign, that which is forgiving, towards beauty, towards kindness, towards gentleness—to become the expression of one's infinite potentiality. And we do this out of an innate devotion to God. I see people all the time that are devoted to God and not even aware that they are. "That's a fact-resist." [True.] Isn't that funny? They're already on their way. They look like a little iron filing and a big powerful magnet is holding them up in the air, and they are worrying about whether they are going to get there or not. I have to laugh at it because they are obviously suspended.

It's because we're powerfully attracted by our infinite potential that we're here. Some lecture someplace, some meditation someplace, some workbook, some mantra, some form of worship. One of the best forms of worship is integrity. Integrity is a way of worshiping God. It's a way of acknowledging God in ordinary life. How can I best honor God, except by doing the best carpentry I can do? And I'm all nicked up from recent carpentry. So, just to make a little storeroom is nothing, except that you want it to be the best little storeroom you can make out of the available materials, time, etc. To be integrous, then, to be integrous within oneself benefits all of mankind. To be integrous is a way of worshiping God. To bring integrity to the workplace. You see because your integrity influences everybody else.

And the new measure of success is going to be integrity. That's a whole new paradigm. That's the emergence of *Homo spiritus*. The book I'm finishing now, we talk about the emergence of *Homo spiritus*—a new emergence on the evolutionary tree. And I think *Homo spiritus* is going to require a different nervous system. Once you get over 500–600, it's tough. "There is, in actuality, the emergence of *Homo spiritus*-resist." [True.] "There is an actual new branch off the evolutionary tree-resist." [True.] "It will eventuate into—we have permission." [True.] "The evolution of the nervous system itself-resist." [True.] "This nervous system is not made for over 600-resist." [True.] Yeah, this nervous system is not made for over 600. So, if mankind is going to keep hanging into the physical domain and having a physical body, and at the same time, evolving spiritually, there's a point where some better apparatus is required.

* * *

So the late '80s then, was to me, you know, the prophecy about the second coming of Christ. Well, because people think of themselves as bodies, they expect a physicality to appear and announce itself as the return of Jesus. "I think the emergence of consciousness over 200 was the anlage of the emergence of Christ consciousness-resist." [True.] "The return of Christ to the earth, then, would be signaled by the crossing over from that which is ungodly to that which is Godly-resist." [True.]

So, to me, the second coming of Christ means the reemergence of Christ consciousness as becoming progressively dominant within the human domain. See, because that which is benevolent and loving is kind, and kindness means not to shock people. You understand, if I was capable of influencing the evolution of human consciousness, it would be to bring it slowly and progressively and even ever more pleasurably, exquisitely, delightfully, joyfully into manifestation, and not just *bam!* You know what I mean? Because you've got to get used to it.

You have to get used to a calmer, more peaceful, more loving—it's shocking to people. It's shocking to yourself, even, when you suddenly make a giant leap in consciousness, and suddenly you're almost stunned by the beauty and the silence and the Presence of God as Love with an intensity beyond which one could even imagine. The Presence of God as infinite Love is overwhelming, and it does take you out of the world. Anybody who's seriously committed to spiritual work, I always tell them to be sure your relatives know what you're up to, or your friends or somebody; because at any moment one can go into a state that cannot be conveyed, described. One becomes speechless; motion is almost impossible. In higher states, you become weak. Everything is slowed down. You forget about eating. You forget about all physical things. So, you need somebody to know that you're a spiritually committed person. And, if you go into a silent state of bliss, it doesn't need

A New Paradigm of Reality

shock treatment. It doesn't need a shot of Thorazine. You can suggest he eat some soup, but you may not get much of an answer to it.

Spiritual work is very serious work. It can bring about *profound* changes, both physically and within one's sense of reality, sense of self. It can change profoundly, and in an instant, with no forewarning. More usually one begins to feel joy more often and notice the beauty of things that you didn't notice before. There are certain sort of warnings coming up in advance. You notice how beautiful everyone is. You tend to fall in love with everything. There's that "falling in love" phase where you fall in love with all of life and everything in it and everyone. And that's sort of a warning to get your affairs in order. Get your affairs in order—because one is like led to that which you need to be led to. And then, the willingness to surrender even *that* to God, even Ecstasy. Spiritual Ecstasy beyond description comes up to be surrendered "To Thee, O God."

One time I was dancing in front of the altar at midnight in a chapel over here, Chapel of the Holy Cross. They didn't used to lock it; it was open all night. And the candles burned all night, and the music was on all night. And all the visitors had left, and at twelve o'clock or one in the morning, you could go there and meditate, all within this chapel with the candles and music and the beauty, and you would just go into an ecstatic state beyond description. Now they lock it up, turn off the music, and put the lights out—it's the health department or somebody. And such ecstatic states. The ecstatic state was described by Ramakrishna, so after I learned that Ramakrishna went into it, I quit worrying about it. Such ecstatic states.

So, somebody has to tell you that those states are there. They're going to be experienced. If you're being attracted by the ultimate potentiality of the evolution of human consciousness, then you're going to be pulled through those states. And when Ecstasy beyond description, the willingness to surrender even *that* to God—when that's surrendered to God, then the most awesome of all: a peace of such profundity, of such extent and such dimension and of such expression through its quality and its exquisite presence takes the place of Ecstasy. And that gets you beyond 599.

KARMA AND DEVOTION

We told you how to get beyond the 400s, now the 500s. This, you see, the reverence, love, lovingness brings one up to an exquisite joyfulness within which there is a serenity. The revelation of the Presence of God and a transfiguration takes place within the person. You will never be the same again. To have experienced the Presence of God, it is not possible to go back, huh? Then, up here are the states—this is just Joy, but up here should be Ecstasy. Out of Joy, man moves on to an Ecstasy that's beyond description. Beyond comprehension.

That exquisite bliss, that ecstatic ecstasy, the willingness to surrender even that to God brings an infinite state which is all-prevailing, which is the Absolute Reality that prevails. And in due time, one can go back into the world and be alive to the world without its being disturbed at all. The state is always present. Then one witnesses what was the person; the persona returns to interact with the world if that's one's karmic propensity. One may or may not return to the world. Most do not. Most, once you hit that state of peace—that's it. One is finished with the world. And there is no obligation to remain, but for unknown karmic reasons, one may stay. In that case, the persona is given permission to reactivate within the world, to respond to the world in a way the world comprehends within their dimensions of reality and learns to refunction in the world.

By that time, one has located spiritual teachers that are aware of such conditions. And I think it is a duty of the teacher always to warn, to educate about what these states are, how they come about, to know that it's all right. It's all right to feel bliss and ecstasy, and it's all right to let the body fall over. If it ceases to breathe, then it's immaterial. One is not obligated to breathe it again. Some people rebreathe it when it stops breathing, out of a sense of obligation. So, at that point one releases that sense of obligation and becomes detached. You are not obliged to the world nor anyone in it. So, that's one of the last attachments one lets go.

On the way of spiritual progression, seeing as this is a class of people who are destined for the Ultimate, or they wouldn't be here—we already reaffirmed that. Along the way . . . especially when you get into the 500s, you begin to pull up that which is opposed to spirituality, which is threatened by it, and one has to watch that benevolence and lovingness does not take the form of naivete and ignorance and fall back into a different ignorance. To be loving but at the same time guard the gates. There's a certain phase in the 500s where one becomes the target of that which is nonintegrous. They see your vulnerability. There's a certain phase in that level where you cannot see anything but love. And so, one has to still preserve integrity. So, the safeguard, then, in the 500s—the levels of Love—is still then to recall integrity. Is what they are presenting to you integrous? Because it can be cleverly conveyed, to sell what you know for a price, etc. It comes up as a temptation.

So, I've spoken in previous lectures about the Luciferic temptation of power over others, money, power, fame, and seduction in its various forms. Certain entities will see a person in that blissful state of lovingness as vulnerable. One's protection, then, is integrity. It's not loving to allow others to be nonintegrous with you. That's confusing "love" with "passivity." It's not of service to yourself or others to allow that which is nonintegrous to have an effect on your life. So, out of integrity, then, we have to let executives go in the name of the business, because for the business to survive, it has to be based on the rock of integrity, which will survive success. Without integrity, you cannot survive success.

So, we've talked enough this morning about the evolution of consciousness, because as it manifests as yourself; you personalize it. But, what you're personalizing, itself, is not personal. It's consciousness, and you're merely calling it "me" or "myself," but that's just what you're calling it. So, when you see that you're just calling it that, and innately it's neither "this" nor "that" nor "here" nor "there," one realizes that what is speaking is consciousness itself. What is presenting itself to your own awareness is the Divinity within expressing itself as the joy of one's own existence. The source of joy, then, is the awareness of the Presence of God within as one's own existence.

KARMA AND DEVOTION

If you can't find God, all you have to do is turn this music on and do nothing else when you hear the essence of the exquisite Presence expressing itself as beauty and infinite compassion. The way to God is extremely radical, at times. Pick up a prayer here, a hymn there, attend a workshop here, read a book there: "I can't figure out; I can't seem to make any progress." One finds that which is sympatico with oneself, and then *persists* with it with a *dogged* determination, an absolute commitment beyond all commitments. If you find it through this music, you play this music around the clock, now and forever more. You don't need to eat; you don't have to go to the bathroom; you don't have to go anywhere; you don't have to answer the phone.

There comes a time when you decide to make "the run for it." It can be a mantra, it can be a meditation, it could be meditating on a guru, it can be something you consider divine, sacred, and you go with it, *no matter what*. And, if you don't eat after a couple of weeks and death faces you, so you die. So? That's the least of it. Dying is a snap! It's the coward's way out; it's taken by everybody.

Can you get to heaven by dying? No, you get there by a fixity of focus and a determination. It's an act of the Spiritual Will. It is by an act of the Spiritual Will that you've already chosen your future. And that's why you're here.

I got a letter the other day. It says, "I've read the first six pages of the preface, and I have to talk to you right away." I mean, it was adorable, you know. You get deluged with all the forms of communication that are existent nowadays. The fax goes round the clock; the e-mail never stops; the computer never stops; the telephone never stops; the answering machine never stops; the answering service never stops. It's not possible to answer it all. And I read everything, and I sort of mentally communicate an answer. It's not possible within the physical domain to handle it. First of all, I can't type. The office has bought a computer, and I can't find the On switch. I'm not lying. On my computer there's no On or Off switch. Because I couldn't get beyond that point, I gave it up. I mean, if you can't even find the On–Off switch, Doc, you know it's not for you, you know what I'm saying? It's not in your dimension,

A New Paradigm of Reality

somehow. I just want to apologize to all the people that have sent such beautiful communications, and I cannot answer them all.

The answers to most of the questions that people send are already within the written material or the visuals. I try to include everything that could possibly come up, so that if a thing is not understood, it hasn't been meditated on, that's all. You haven't looked at it long enough. And most questions, I feel like saying, "Well, look at it and call me back in twenty years." It's like, as you focus on a situation mentally, and ask for God's help to resolve it, ask to see it differently, ask for the miraculous, pray to the Holy Spirit, and rattle the gates of heaven; when it's karmically allowed, you suddenly see it. You suddenly see the answer, and it resolves itself.

So spiritual work is different than intellectual work. Intellectual work is asking a specific question and then getting a specific answer, and now you feel satisfied, which is too bad. The actual answer comes from reflecting on a thing. So, we talk during these lectures about how the style of a spiritually committed person becomes more and more contemplative, so that all that arises, one more or less contemplates. And that way, one will eventually bypass the polarities. "Isn't peace good, and isn't war awful?" No. War is terrific. And peace is terrific. Frankly, they are actually the same. Except, to the observer, they look like opposites. Right now, the country's involved in a situation. Should we be pacifists or activists? Should we be reactive or proactive? That's what it really comes down to. People who are old enough remember World War II and what went on at that time. So those who have not learned from history are condemned to repeat it, huh? I remember the prime minister of England taking a pacifist position with Adolph Hitler. He says, "He's an okay guy; all we have to do is this, that, and the other." Right? So, you cannot confuse passivity with peace, because very often passivity brings war. I lived through the era in which passivity brought the death of 70 million people.

In 1929, the new secretary of state was Stimson, I believe. We had an intelligence service, of course, during World War I, and then it continued after World War I. And his first day in office, as secretary of state, the intelligence service presented its report for the day to the secretary of state, who said, quote: "Gentlemen do not read other gentlemen's mail." That cost us another 70 million people dead. Cost us Pearl Harbor.

I want to clarify that pacifism is not the same as taking the action that takes you to peace, because peace takes integrity. Integrity does not allow itself to play ball with nonintegrity. Right? Truth is often the courage to stand one's ground and say, "No further, no more." Somebody asked me that question during the intermission. What is the integrous stance? The integrous stance is not to allow your monastery to be ravaged by wolves. You have to protect your monastery.

To transcend the opposites, then, is to stop seeing one thing as one thing, and the other thing as its opposite. One has to be in a very high state to see, like death, war makes no difference. Die by the droves, die singly. Because the evolution of consciousness takes us through these various forms, and you somersault with them, and you go the way of the Tao or you break. When it's time for war, you go with the war. When it's time for peace, you go with the peace. So, what should a person do about it? One should hold an integrous desire for peace and prayer, and then allow Divine Will to express itself in the karmic expression of humankind. How many times do you have to die in war before you see it's absurd? A lot of times, apparently. Over and over and over again, people choose it, yes? Over and over again until people learn that part of spirituality is integrity. *Integrity means to stop playing victim.* It's not integrous to allow your husband to beat you all the time. It's not integrous to allow your children to be abused. It's not integrous to allow people to steal from you.

The illusion that one has to transcend in politics is that other people are like you. I've got news for you: Other people are not like you at all. Other people think you are a stupid idiot. The presumption you see from educated, consciousness level of 430, is to presume that other people are like us: "They wouldn't do that—they'd bring destruction on their own people." Of course they would, and of course they would bring destruction on their own people.

A New Paradigm of Reality

We see it over and over again. The leaders of other countries are not in the same level of consciousness. Megalomania doesn't care if their whole country gets wiped out. It's very hard for sane people to realize the degree of insanity of megalomania. Hitler didn't care if all his people got killed; he thought they deserved it. In fact, what was left standing, he would have eliminated if the generals had followed his orders to burn Berlin to the ground.

The recent dictator out of the Balkans who's on trial in the U.N. Court of Appeals, or whatever it is, the same way. Megalomania is the, you might say, the extreme opposite of what we would imagine Divinity would be. That which comes from the lower astral *hates* humans. "That which is dominated by the lower astral—we have permission to ask-resist." [True.] "Hates humanity-resist." [True.] You're going to put your trust in a dictator of another country that *hates* humanity? Doesn't hate *you*; it hates its own people. The megalomania is not satisfied until you're wiped out and also his country. He wants *all* of mankind destroyed. Remember there was an era there during the Communist era when they were planning the mega bomb—that if they lost the war, would eliminate all of human life. Therefore, to be spiritual doesn't mean to be foolish or blind or go into denial and sacrifice needlessly. However, everything that mankind goes through serves an ultimate lesson. And we go through the same lesson over and over until we *get* it. We can't hand the keys to the car to a drinking alcoholic, who is also psychotic and off his meds, because you're "spiritual." No, folks, it won't happen that way. It doesn't. So, there's one of the lessons we learn along the spiritual pathway is that naivete is different than ignorance, and that's different from innocence. And they are all different than denial. What passes as spirituality is often denial. A posturing ignorance. An assumed innocence, which innocence itself does not need to assume. Just like humility does not have to assume the position of pseudo-humility. The goody-goody side of spirituality is available everywhere. The goody-goody side of spirituality has a big trap to it; otherwise, everybody would be enlightened. If it's easy to skyrocket to 1000, everybody would be there. We'd all be off this planet, turn it back to the dinosaurs.

KARMA AND DEVOTION

They know what to do with it. Kill each other without being pious about it. They were honest. "You look good; I'm going to eat you, and I'm going to kill you, okay?" I mean, no pretense. You know, "He's just an innocent good fellow, and if we all prayed for him, *Tyrannosaurus rex* will become like the rest of us." *Tyrannosaurus rex* will not become like the rest of us, because he's run by energies from a different domain.

So, part of being spiritual is starting to become integrous. It requires honesty and strength. Part of the spiritual is the spiritual warrior, who stands up and defends the truth. Bin Laden is not going to become a good guy and change his mind; it ain't gonna be. The enemies of that which we have, are enemies because they hate that which we have and that which we are. Why does the lower astral hate humanity? It's because humanity has the chance to return to God and they do not. "The hatred that emerges on this planet stems from the lower astral realms-resist." [True.] Stems from the lower astral. "It stems from that which hates mankind-resist." [True.] "It stems from that which would like to destroy mankind." [True.] "Would like to destroy God." [True.] "And destroy all who seek God." [True.] So, that should take care of naivete. You're not exactly walking amongst friends every moment of every day.

That which hates God seeks to dominate and *did* dominate until the late 1980s. The consciousness of mankind was below 200. That which hates God, let's say, really dominated the consciousness of mankind until the 1980s. Only now are we crossing over where integrity has a chance. Before I turn over the cards and my checkbook to somebody, I want to see his credit rating. Is that not spiritual? No, that's spiritual. Pseudo-spiritual is: "Oh, I trust everybody. I'm sure I can give anybody my checkbook and the keys to my car. And I know I can depend on him to return it." I've got news for you—I had to go down, after waiting a month, to Cottonwood and get my car because it was still sitting in the driveway, because he was on a bender. I would never have gotten my car back if I had waited for the goodness of mankind to blossom through this idiot! So being spiritual doesn't mean being a stupid pussy willow. I say that because naive pussy willows get taken, they get taken, and not just financially; they get taken spiritually: "I got a new guru for you."

So, that which is deleterious to the true pathway loves to snare the really committed spiritual seeker, and what's his downside? His downside is his naivete. Therefore, as a teacher, it's my responsibility to get off the sweet pussy willow path of flowers and hearts and hymns and get with it that you've got to be real to be spiritual. You have to be able to accept the reality of how it is and not get into pretense. A lot of prayer is just pretenseful. You can pray up a storm for bin Laden all you want. He doesn't want to *go* where you want to go. If he wanted to go where you want to go, he wouldn't be aligned with the lower astral forces. You understand? He wouldn't be there.

[Q]: "*The energy of the teacher, the guru, can it advance your consciousness or undo negative karma?*"

Let's see. "We have permission to answer that." [True.] "The answer is 'yes.'" [True.] Hmm, I didn't know that. "The presence of the teacher being aligned with God, not the teacher, undoes the negative karma-resist." [True.] Okay. Yes, because of one's devotion to God, one seeks a teacher. It's because of one's devotion to God that the acting it out within the physical domain releases the negative karma. That's true.

"Much of the effect of the teacher is vibrational-resist." [True.] It's the effect of the teacher on one's consciousness that's strictly vibrational. "It's strictly the energy of the field-resist." [True.] "It's impersonal-resist." [True.] "It's the power of Divinity through the vibrational energy of the karmic field that's expressing itself, I see, oh, I see, in the Atmic body-resist." [True.] Oh, okay. Yes, the energy field, then, of the teacher vibrates one's own aura, picks it up. I remember consciously picking it up from the Karmapa. I saw the Karmapa once many years ago, and I just "got" the vibrational field. It had nothing to do with the Karmapa—it had to do with the vibrational field, but I caught it at that instant. You were catching it before, too, when we were into the music together.

KARMA AND DEVOTION

Divinity is available everywhere. The recognition of it as beauty is a constant opportunity. To reach God, one tunes in on beauty, listens to beauty. The sound of God is silent. The sound of God is present at all times. Behind the talkingness, behind the noise is a profound and infinite silence, in which is the presence, so powerful that one has to resist it in order to keep functioning in the world. So, beautiful music like that will take you right out; you have to sit down. It takes you right out of it because of the vibration and the beauty. So, in the high 500s, it becomes sometimes very difficult to function, because one is crying all the time, and every little thing that's beauty just knocks you out. You have to stay away from kitties; they blow you away. You have to stay away from lovers; people that are in love, they're terrible. One time I almost missed a plane. I was sitting there waiting for the plane, and this couple looked at each other, and wow, you could just see the love there. I almost did not make the plane. I had to bring myself back.

"There's various kinds of hell." [True.] "There's different dimensions of hell." [True.] "So, there are different hells." [True.] "The hell that I was in, you still had a chance-resist." [True.] Oh, thank you, Lord. I guess if you're even kind to one simple little beetle, you get to experience hell, but with the chance for salvation, because I don't think there's much deeper levels than I was at. Let's see. "We *can* discuss this-resist." [True.] Okay. "The level of this experience was about as low as it gets-resist." [True.] Wow. "And others have to stay there forever?" [True.]

People joke about hell, fool around with hell, and basically people are scared to death of it, and with good reason, because it's worse than your wildest imagination of how awful it can be. One's worst imagination is merely the frosting on the top. From there, it becomes staggeringly worse, nor is there any chance of hope anywhere. In fact, it even says on the way down, "Abandon hope." That artist who wrote that, Dante—I don't know how he knew that. But there it is, and it's very, very visible. "Abandon all hope." And, when you go beyond hopelessness, there's a realm unimaginable. And yet there still remained that chance at that

A New Paradigm of Reality

level. And I said, "If there is a God, I ask Him to help me." The next experience was a shining forth of the Presence of God as Allness. In sheer brilliance, exquisite, self-revealing, wordless, silent, ever-present. The quality of Divinity is stunning. It is All That Is; it includes all that is and is one's reality, beyond time, beyond "then" or "now." I think we spoke that "now" is an illusion, the same as "past" and "future." There is no "now" any more than there's a "then" or a "to be." The reality is an always-ness. A forever always-ness, which is one's reality. The celestial realms are more like that music. The music takes you really into a celestial realm. "Heavenly" is to be in the exquisite state that that music takes you to, and never have to leave it. One can just be in a state of exquisite joy, endlessly, because "always" is always until one elects to leave it for some reason.

There are certainly pitfalls in this, so we wanted to be sure and mention them. The seduction of the innocent. So, the danger of the 500s—the danger of the 400s, we've already discussed: endless thinkingness, confusing abstract concepts with reality where it's actually only a concept. The 500s—I've already discussed with you the downside of the 500s: to get into denial—that all we have to do is be good guys with Mr. Hitler, and he will certainly keep his agreement with us. He will not keep his agreement with us. That which is not integrous does not keep agreements. There's no point in signing peace treaties with somebody who calibrates at 90. He thinks you're an idiot: "I mean, we suckered them in on that one, didn't we?" So, it doesn't mean being a fool. To be spiritual doesn't mean to be a fool.

Let's see. "How does one transcend the fear of one's own extinction?"

Yes, that's a good term for it. One has to be willing to become extinct. To dissolve into nothing. To no longer exist. To surrender existence itself. That's called for, but you won't get to that until the last lecture. I don't want anybody getting enlightened between now and the last lecture, please. You have to be a card-carrying member to cross the last doorway. There are certain confrontations. Along the way, there are confrontations and trials. Spiritual teachings are different. The teachers and the teachings are different. And the downside is different for each of these levels, you see. If you're overcoming fear, then cowardice is going to take you out, isn't it? This is the test to see whether or not you can walk into the bullets and die for your country. Yeah, you're going to walk into the bullets, and you are going to die—that's for sure. And then you shoot right up here, above 200.

When I committed hari-kari in a past life, I remember the experience was agonizing beyond description, agonizing. The pain was far worse than what you can imagine. It was *horrific*. And with an unstoppable will, I went through it and came out ecstatic. To be out of the body was great. The body was agonizing. And I was ecstatic. Ecstatic—never have to face that one again—to overcome fear. So, some of the things that we decry, to decry hari-kari, let's say, but it was called for, so I set up a situation in which that was the only thing that could be done and save one's honor, and I did it. Don't have to do it again. But there isn't any other way. You have to actually walk into the bullets and actually die for your country. You have to actually rip your guts out and die for one's faith.

So, the lessons of spirituality call forth, then, things that seem, within the world, quite extreme. We say, "Oh, that's extreme. Look at all the warriors that had to die." How are they going to transcend that fear of physical death unless you walk right into it? You can't pretend in your mind, "Oh, I won't be afraid of giving up my body for God." Well, we'll see. *Chop!* Too late to change your mind now as the sword goes through your skull. In a split instant, you realize that you've just made it. Ecstatic. I told you about the time that warrior and myself killed each other. Man, we really did it too. Both of us burst into: I killed him for Jesus, and he killed me for Allah. I mean, it was ecstatic; we both went out of body. So, you've got to be willing to go to considerable extremes. Your family will think you're mad. They may call the police, call the psychiatrist.

That was the function I had back east. I was the consultant for the Zen monastery, the Episcopal diocese, the Catholic diocese,

A New Paradigm of Reality

the nuns, various monasteries, and religious retreat centers, etc. Is this guy delusional, or what is his state? Because once you've got that commitment to God, nothing will stop you. They'd say, "Doctor, he's going to whatchamacallit." And I'd say, "Well, yes, let him." "But then he'll die." "That's true." The world thinks in very banal terms: "Why, he's going to die of that." And I'd say, "Right. That's true; he is. That's true; he is." Is he in a state of Ecstasy, or is he catatonic? Is this a person in high Ecstasy, or is this a bipolar manic, into religiosity? Sometimes it's pretty hard to tell.

So, to some degree, we walk near the edge. You push your spiritual commitment to the edge. And, if you go over the edge, so you go over the edge. So what? So, the commitment is a complete and total commitment. When I say, if you can find God through that music, that ecstatic state, don't stop playing it, around the clock all day, every day, now and forever. When you've transcended that music, you can let it go.

So, there comes that time when you make a run for God. There comes the time when your spiritual commitment, you know that *this is it,* that you're not coming back until you get there. And then you make the final run. We'll talk about the final run in my last lecture; otherwise, nobody will be here next time. We'll all be at home meditating, not eating, and listening to music—and the families will be calling the police. "The doctor made me do it. I went to his lecture and . . ." Along the way, one may also get a great number of physical calamities, and aches and pains.

If you look up the mystic in the encyclopedia, it'll give you quotes going back to the 12th, 13th, 14th, 15th centuries of various mystics and their descriptions of what they went through. One said you'll spend more time in your sickbed than you will on your knees. That bringing up negative energies and what's associated with them and the karma that's associated with them may put you through all kinds of strange wracks and experiences, that really you need people who are spiritually advanced and have been through them to reassure you as to what they are. If they seem like a calamity, so? So, it's a calamity.

KARMA AND DEVOTION

[Q]: "How do you reconcile the contention that there is no causality with the assertion that one's karma is the consequence of one's past actions?"

That's an easy question. I mean, it's easy to see how it would arise because of the mind's proclivity to translate everything into causality. You see, one thing doesn't *cause* another. But, in the quantum reality, what's happening is, you're increasing likelihoods of potentialities. "This" is not *causing* "that," but under "this" condition, the likelihood of "this" happening is increased. However, in spiritual evolution, freedom of the will is ever present; otherwise, there would be no karmic merit possible, nor would there be karmic demerit. It's because of Spiritual Will to say yes to God. Apparently, heaven is populated by people who say yes to God. You have to say yes to God to get to heaven. God doesn't want anybody who doesn't want to be there, who hasn't consciously chosen God. That's something I haven't ever asked before. "I have permission to ask it-resist." [True.] "And that's a fact." [True.] "God doesn't want anybody in heaven who doesn't want Him." [True.] Okay, it's simple enough. So, apparently karmic merit comes from having had the opportunity to choose either way, and to have chosen "this" rather than "that." All is happening by free choice, not by causal determination. You see if things were causal, there would be no karmic merit nor demerit, would there? You could just say "this" was caused by something else, or "that" was caused by "that," and "that" was caused by the NBC news, and "that" was caused by the paper, and "that" was caused by what my parents did, so there's no responsibility. Neither is there freedom, neither is there merit, nor is there room for growth. It's only because you have the option to say yes or no, that one, by saying yes, automatically advances one's self. I don't know—I didn't set the whole deal up—don't ask me about it!

[Q]: "How can we learn whether or not we had past lives?"

Well, I suppose you can just ask. Let's see if we have permission to ask. "We have permission to ask." [True.] "We have permission to

A New Paradigm of Reality

ask about the person who wrote this-resist." [True.] "This person did have past human lifetimes-resist." [True.] Yes. You can ask—that's the easiest way. We said the likelihood is that everybody in the room had, what did we say? About 25, on an average, about 25 lifetimes. When you get to a certain level, you remember them. You start to remember them; you begin to suspect them.

There are people who specialize in past-life regression. You know, they can take you back there, and you reexperience it. People get it through dreams, hallucinations, and various other ways. You begin to suspect it. I mean, it's not necessary to know, not necessary to know. As I said, you could skip this whole lecture and reach God in an instant, ha! As soon as you walk out of here—*bam!* Your spouse will know it, because she'll say, "Where am I?" Uh-oh. God shock.

That was another one they used to bring me. Is this monk in God shock? It's God shock. You hit unexpectedly a high satori, and it totally blows you away—disoriented, you don't know how to function in the world; you're confused, can't think. There's a very major change. And there is actually a period of time when you can't function. So, have a good place to go away when you reach that state. Pick a nice place in the country and tell them, "If I stop talking and eating and have a silly grin on my face, let's just go there, and we'll have chicken soup once a week."

[Q]: "How can we surrender everything to God?"

The willingness to surrender to God is sort of a catch-22, because there is a love for God that is so *deep* within yourself, so *profound*, so exquisitely intense, that, for God, one would surrender anything. It's something to be discovered. It's there; that capacity, that willingness to surrender everything to God is innate within consciousness. When you need it and call it forth, it's there. Would I be willing to surrender "this" to God? Yes. Then you get to a tough one.

So, innate to the pathway of nonduality or the Zen bare-bones ascetic route, aligned with it, is the way of the heart. It is only out of devotion to God, out of love for God; it's only because of the heart, that you're willing to follow the pathway of negation, let's

KARMA AND DEVOTION

say. Out of your love for God, you are willing to let go of a positionality. So, one lets go of the trite ideas of "right and wrong," "war is bad," "peace is good." More crime goes on in peaceful times than in war. In war, people are too busy to commit crimes, and when the war is over, then they go back to it.

There's a willingness to surrender all presumptions of the mind and ask God for revelation. It's like one holds one's positionality and asks God to resolve it out of the willingness to surrender it to God. So, the willingness to surrender things to God comes out of devotion. When you get into a really incredibly high place of beauty, you'll realize you can get in touch with it there. In the state that you're in, you'd be willing to surrender anything to God, everything to God, life itself. And in the last instant, that is what is asked for. Are you willing to surrender your life itself to God?

So, the more you clear away the ego through, let's say the Buddhism side of spirituality or the Advaita side of nonduality, it strengthens the way of the heart, the traditional Christian way, let's say, through the heart. The more you evolve through the heart, the greater power you have to let go positionalities that are deeply ingrained. So, each one assists the other. To be devoted to one's spiritual work, you're doing that out of your love for God. The reason to become enlightened is out of your love for God. That's the reason. "It is out of my love for Thee, O Lord, that I do surrender all that I think and believe that I am, including life itself. To Thee, O Lord, do I surrender my being."

That's an act of the Spiritual Will. It comes from the heart of the Spiritual Will. It comes out of connecting with the inner Joy. When you connect with the inner Joy, it gives you the spiritual power to surrender anything else except Truth to the Lord, yeah. The worship of God, the love for God, the devotion to God, the love and devotion to spiritual work itself is a sacrifice and a gift to God, who doesn't need any gifts; it's just a style of speech. It's a gift of love, a gift of love, and it is its own reward, just like you follow something that brings you great joy and ecstasy, and you tell somebody about it. And then, one day you can just tell by the look on their face that they "got it." The look on their face

A New Paradigm of Reality

that they "got it" brings you such joy that it is its own reward; it's self-fulfilling. Nothing more is needed.

Compassion for oneself arises out of seeing one's own innocence. Intrinsically, the innate, that which is within oneself, is innocent. Out of the Unmanifest arises the manifest. Out of the manifest arises consciousness and the spirit of God as life. Life itself is innocent. It takes whatever form. It stays life; it does not change with the form.

To truly love oneself, then, it's necessary to love God, and to love God, it's really necessary to love oneself. So, we constantly let go any blocks to the realization of the truth of that. The willingness to be compassionate, the willingness to surrender all to God. In the end, it's a matter of trust and faith. And in the end, when you are asked to walk off the cliff—in the end, you can walk off the cliff, and it's the faith and trust in the teachers—the veracity of the teachers, the energy field of their vibration, the absolute conviction of the truth of the Buddha and all the great Avatars. At the last moment, when one is asked to give up the Self, life, and all that you know exists, then up comes that devotion of enormous power. One would let oneself be eaten alive if God asked you to. "For Thee O Lord, do I give myself." You surrender even life itself to Thee, O Lord.

The juices of illness and negativity and suffering are the "suffering" itself. In other words, people look for psychological reasons—there's a naivete, you see it every night on television—sort of pop psychology. Well, this guy just shot 14 strangers in a row. "What do you suppose happened in his childhood?"—that's the first thing, you know. Nothing! Nothing that happened in his childhood has got anything to do with what he's doing now. That's just a plausible rationalization. We like to psychologize things because that gives us a superior feeling that we understand them and can explain them, when the truth is, all these explanations are nonsensical and have nothing to do with it. "You know why I like shooting people? Because I like shooting people, you understand?" The payoff *is* the experience itself. Not, "Because I'm getting even with my father from childhood when he abused me," and all that. Even if that's a fact, it's still got nothing to do with why you are doing what you do now. You do what you do now because the experience *itself* is the payoff. The experience itself is what is sought. Once we seek to feel sorry for ourselves, we seek to feel resentments and revenge. We love to seethe with rage and indignation. Isn't that fun? We just seethe. Oh, we hate them! Grrr! Let's just have a hate parade. I mean, people just *dig* hate, you know.

You watch those news broadcasts from the Middle East, as I've spoken before. Watch the expressions on their faces as they throw rocks at each other. Man, they're really getting off on it. I mean, they're having a ball. They just love it. And you want to get in there with a peace sign? Get out of there! Who wants peace? In the middle of a prize fight, somebody runs out there with a peace sign? Give us a break!

[Q]: "How does one surrender the will to think?"

That is sort of a tricky one. And we've said that thinkingness is its own reward. We just got through saying that the reason behind, see, because that's based on causality, and there is no such thing as causality, so looking for the cause of something, you always end up with a tautology, chasing your tail. The payoff of the experience *is* the experience. *That* is the payoff. The payoff of hating is to get to experience "hating." One can retrospectively justify it: "My father was cruel to me," etc., but that, frankly, is not why you are doing what you're doing now, because you are not five years old; that's not your father; it's got nothing to do with it. You're violent right now because you enjoy being violent.

I've got 50 girls, many of whom just enjoy being violent. They like to hit cement walls with theirs fists and fracture their bones. Is logic or reason or psychology going to find a reason? You hear them try to find it. And I humor them and say, "Uh-huh." You hit your fist against the cement so you can break your fist and say, "Look, I broke my fist against the cement wall. See how crazy I am." I think, "Look, I know you're crazy enough; you don't have to prove it. You don't have to break bones to tell me you're crazy." But what she's saying to me is "I am *that* crazy. I'm so crazy that I'll

A New Paradigm of Reality

actually break my bones against a cement wall." I said to her, "You know, I get it, I get it. Yes, you *are* that crazy." Oh, dear.

The payoff of an experience is the experience itself. Therefore, the only thing you have to sacrifice is your desire for that experience. We indulge in certain fantasies and feelings and recollections and memories, because of that which it brings up. And we're doing it for the sake of that which it brings up. And, thereby, the ego ensures its own survival, through sheer repetition. We get addicted to being addicting. One of the things you've got to let go of is wanting to become addicted. We're addicted to thinking; we're addicted to suffering; we're addicted to guilt; we're addicted—one of the things you have to detach from is the desire to become addicted to things. Not addicted to this, not addicted to that, but becoming addicted to addiction itself. Becoming attached to attachment itself. Some people become attached to everything constantly. They're just attached to everything; you just watch them. They're attached to this, they're attached to that, attached to their thoughts, attached to their habits; they're attached to everything. Attached to their possessions.

You have to let go not being attached to money or attached to greed, attached to sex, whatever. You have to let go wanting to be attached, period. What do I get out of feeling attached to things? Whatever they might be. Attachment itself, then, is some kind of a security operation, operating out of illusion. So, in spiritual work, you try to find a common denominator, so that when you let go of "this" down here, it lets go a whole lot of things because you don't have enough time to let go all the blocks and impediments. What you can find is a commonality. Defuse that commonality and now whole rafts of things leave your mind and never come back there anymore.

* * *

There is a certain parallelism between the nonlinear and linear domain, between spirituality and physicality. Therefore, that which is legitimately spiritual may also have its parallel within the physical domain. The fact that there is a parallel in which you can imitate the spiritual by physical manipulation, it's a non sequitur to conclude, therefore, that the spiritual is unreal, because it can be imitated within the physical. All kinds of experiences can be imitated by poking various parts of the brain. All kinds of events can be imitated, spuriously created, and I suppose Indian rope tricks can be performed. Umm. There is a limited parallelism, in which that which is the imitation within the physical domain has, to the unsophisticated, a superficial appearance to the real.

One way to differentiate the truth of the two is by calibration. We've said that out-of-body experiences, for instance, are quite amazing and fun besides. How many here have had out-of-body experiences? Yeah, okay. If we calibrate the energy of the entity—the "person," before and after. . . . I think we've done this before. "Out-of-body experience, the person's calibration does not really change significantly. We have permission to ask that." [True.] "It remains about the same-resist." [True.] "But you do learn something." [True.] "You learn that you are more than a physical body-resist." [True.]

So, on your deathbed, severely ill, critically ill, gravely ill, never even heard of out-of-body experience. Next thing you know, you're six feet in the air, weightless, invisible. Fantastic! Free as a bird. If you think, "Over there," you're over there. You think, "Here," you're here—great! No time wasted in traveling. "This consciousness advanced as a result of that experience-resist." [Not true.] No. Why not? That's curious. Oh, I see. "The mind discards it as being unreal-resist." [True.] Oh, I see, okay. The reason we don't really grow from it is because the mind doesn't really believe it; it discards it; even while it's going on, you don't believe it. Ha, out of body is strange, isn't it?

Near-death is something else again. That's transformative. And the person's level of consciousness after a near-death experience shows a rather dramatic increase. Many people's lives change incredibly. A number of well-known authors who had near-death experiences describe the total transformation that occurred to them as a result of those kinds of experiences. So that which imitates the spiritual does not show—so, that which imitates a miracle,

A New Paradigm of Reality

the calibrated consciousness of it is, let's say, 190. Very often people who want to disprove the reality of spirituality are people who hate God, and they really come from very low numbers. So that which imitates a miracle doesn't negate the fact that the miraculous occurs. Not only does it occur, but it occurs very frequently and commonly. It's just that ordinary perception doesn't read it because it's outside its paradigm of reality. I used to be in the presence of the miraculous all the time. There was a period of time in which the miraculous was continuous. And people would sit down in that field and walk up healed, and you would see a relative saying, "Well, I told you all along you didn't need that cane." The lady could now walk, and she couldn't walk before, but ordinary consciousness didn't even read what it was. This lady was suddenly able to walk and perfectly fine, you know. You witness the miraculous. People that are not aligned with God—they don't even see it. They don't even see it for what it. . . . Anyway, there's a lot of programs on TV in which professional debunkers love to try to disprove the reality of spiritual phenomena.

I'm not talking about occult. Occult is something else. And generally, we advise people to avoid the supernatural, the occult, the weird, the strange channelings of "Baba This" and "Baba That" from the other side. And people do all kinds of astral tricks. It's best to avoid them.

The sacred, that which is tried and true. Spiritual truth is clear and obvious. You don't really have to study it. That which is peace and love, committed to truth, integrity, surrendering all to God, is the same throughout all of time and all religions, and nothing else is really needed. All a teacher can do is be like a coach, you see, a coach to affirm the validity of the teaching. Anything that varies from that is not of God. Anything that tells you, "Kill infidels for God," is not of God. Not of God. Besides that, you don't really need to know anything.

The false teachers—we've advised about that too. That's another responsibility of the teacher. A true teacher is not interested in money, position, trappings, ownership, possessions, organizations, hierarchies, titles, organizations, treasuries, the

KARMA AND DEVOTION

owning of anything, the possession of anything, the proclaiming of anything. There is only the speaking of the truth as one has come to know it through one's own inner experience, to share that which has been validated through one's own consciousness. Anything else is an artifice.

This willingness to turn things over to God's Will is partly, is a result, you see, of your own Spiritual Will. We described the technique where anything and everything that happens, no matter what, you stop resisting it and you surrender it to God. The news says, "We're all going to war." So, you surrender it to God. *"No, God, we don't want war! Where's my peace sign, Mother?"* Get off it. Without war, how are people ever going to get beyond war? The only way to get beyond war is to get beyond war. You can't just do it out of a textbook in fourth grade. "War is bad for people." That should end war, shouldn't it? If that ended war, there wouldn't be any more. No. People have to go through the gut-rending, ripping experience of devastation.

What amazes me is the extent to which the ego has to go before it relents. It's just amazing, the degree, the extent at which the ego will go. The extremes, barbaric, insane, psychotic degrees, before it finally lets go of a thing. If there's anything I'm dismayed about the human condition, *that* is what it is. I'm dismayed that it takes so much to bring the ego to the level of letting go. Why does it have to be *so* extreme? That distresses me still. So, that is something I will have to let go in myself, that identification with the human condition. Why should it go to such *extremes?* Why does it have to go so *far?* Why does the pain have to be so *bad?* Why does agony have to take you to the pit beyond which no more agony is bearable? And yet, you have to experience more. Why is it so extreme? I don't know. I asked the question today. So, that's my question for the day: Why does it have to be so extreme? Why does human suffering have to be so enormous? Why does it take 70 million people ripped to death by bullets and guns and savage wounds, and their arms and legs being ripped off and exploded into nothingness? Not once, but over and over again. Seventy million in one war. Twenty years later, we got 70 million going in another war. Every 10 or 20 years, another 10, 20, 30, 40, 50, 70 million people go. Why does it take such an extreme? Why is it so severe?

What does it take for people to wake up and recognize a megalomaniac when he's staring you right in the face? Over and over and over again, whole nations march to some megalomaniac's maniac ego. And they don't recognize it for what it is. Why is that? It's presented to them over and over again within one lifetime. They fall for it one time; 20 years later, they fall for it again. Ten years later, they fall for it again. Innately, innately stupid. Well, I guess we say the ego is innately stupid. It really is dumb, isn't it? It really is dumb. So, that's the answer—thank you, Lord. "People are just stupid." "Oh, okay." There are a few. I guess we are dumb, Lord. So, that's why the Buddha said to become enlightened. Unless you grow, you go around and around endlessly in this karmic cycle.

[Q]: *"If you reach enlightenment, is it true you don't have to reincarnate?"*

As far as I know, that's true, yes, if you transcend personal karma. But don't forget one does not transcend the karmic reality of Divinity, that that which is God is the totality of all that exists, and you may escape your own personal karma and go into a very neat place, but you still have not escaped, let's say, the reality. The Allness that exists is the karmic unity of God.

So, I've told you about that Luciferic trap that you hit when you get into a very high place, where you know you are beyond personal karma. And then this Luciferic knowingness comes to you; it's nonverbal: "Now that you are beyond personal karma, you know there is no God to answer for, answer to, there is nothing and no one to answer to for anything, nor are you accountable because there is no personal self that could be accountable." On a certain level of understanding, that certainly sounds true. If there's no personal self, then what would be accountable, and to whom? One is free of all accountability—and is the Luciferic temptation at that level 840 or something. Own that, and you have unlimited power over everyone. You have unlimited power

KARMA AND DEVOTION

over the world. That's the Luciferic temptation. Now that you're beyond all personal karma and accountability, and there is no awful God to punish you for anything anyway; that was all just an imagination in your ego's brain, which you have now let go of; all power is yours. That's the Luciferic temptation. You're all destined for the ultimate, so it will come to you too. Don't say I didn't warn you. "I want my money back; you didn't tell me about that!" I'm telling you now.

It's interesting, but the truth that you've heard from gurus, Krishna, or whoever, walks into that space, there's a knowingness, not a voice, no script, nothing. There's a knowingness that that temptation is in error. It's an error of context. At the time, you're not conscious of what the error is, but there is a refusal, there's a refusal, and then one passes those gates. So, the levels that we see on the board, the higher levels, are guarded by gates. At each gate there is a question, and so I want everybody to know the right answers. God looks at your report card. He says, "You got that one right!" Power over everybody—that's a sucker's game.

* * *

Religion is a fascinating subject, and of course, I look into various aspects of it. In the study of consciousness itself, how it evolved in the form of religion and the difficulties that religions present. I think the purest spiritual pathway is the fastest way to God, and religions can offer a great deal of help along the way: that which is positive about the religion, the fellowship, the beauty, the lovingness of the group, the integrity of the teacher. And I love going to church myself.

[Q]: "When a person declares a spiritual intention, is there a counterforce?"

Is there a counterforce? I'm glad you asked that. Yes, there is a counterforce. There is a counterforce. And it's imperative to discover what the counterforce is. The counterforce can be quite operative, quite effective; and yet, in and of itself, be a snap to let go of once

A New Paradigm of Reality

you find it. You can hold back a whole locomotive, you know, with your finger on this button here. Four thousand tons of locomotive can't move. One little finger, half an ounce—the locomotive can't move, immobilized, the whole steam engine, with one little finger. So, that's not force. It's the knowingness. So, you may discover something in yourself that's really driving you crazy, and it's really countered by a very small understanding, that little subtle understanding. Once you get that, the whole thing clears away of its own. Don't be impressed by how difficult a problem *seems* to be, because its answer is usually very simple. The light switch is on this side, not that side, and you go, "Oh?" That's all it was. Many of the major ones that I bypassed in my life were really that simple. But what they depended on was a willingness to trust, a willingness to trust, to let go of what you think you've got for what you're told will work, you see. So, there's a certain amount of trust in letting go. But you're right, whatever commitment there is to move in this direction, it does tend to be set up. We tried to cover that when we covered the structure of the ego, when we talked about the alternatives and the contraries and the opposites that within yourself, things are set up as opposites.

I have outpatients, and they're afraid they may burst out in the middle of church with a curse or a vulgar word. That's a very frequent obsession with obsessives. They're afraid that in church, they're going to suddenly blurt out a four-letter word right in the middle of Mass. So, that which is holy and sacred, then brings forth its opposite of that which is anti-sacred or whatever you would call it—a blasphemy or something. They would suddenly blurt out something horrible in the middle of church. I suppose we should have a special service for them some Sunday in which they are free to express themselves, and we will all clap and parade and thank them for their honesty and forthrightness and the willingness to share.

* * *

Yes, without love, where would we be? At the bottom of the sea. It takes, you know, a whole slew of people to make these events

KARMA AND DEVOTION

happen. We keep them secret, however. Such pearls are hard to find. We will not reveal them until the last lecture. But it takes 12 or 15 people working around the clock—an enormous amount of energy and work to bring together the communications from so many people; to try to put what we say into a form available to others and distribute them around the world. And it's a great deal of work and energy. And, as I say, I may keep them secret until the last session.

I want to say a few things about kinesiology itself and not to get carried away with it. Kinesiology is just a tool, a useful thing. And a lot of times we use it more for curiosity than for anything, you know, really genuine. You know how people ask about other realms and all—I mean, it's got nothing to do with your enlightenment, you know what I mean? It's just spiritual wandering, you know. So, you stick to your own straightforwardness. All that you know has already been spoken and revealed. It hasn't changed since; it hasn't changed for thousands of years. That which was said today, that which Krishna taught—they're all the same. Because anybody who has ever experienced the Truth, it always comes back forth, exactly the same, because there is only one Truth, and unembellished by thinkingness, the experience is always the same. It manifests itself in the same way. It speaks in the same way. And one can tell at a glance at a sentence or two of a book written by somebody whether they experienced it or not. It's just in the energy of the sentence itself. It's a way of being with it. There's a conviction that comes only from the validity of the experience itself. So, the ultimate Truth is the ultimate, beyond even experiencing.

We've said there's thinkingness; there's that which witnesses the thinkingness; there's that which experiences the witnessing of the thinkingness, until finally one gets to the substrate, which is consciousness itself. And then, if karmically destined, one goes even beyond consciousness itself. Out of that which you are arises consciousness. Hm. So the Truth, the absolute ultimate Truth of that which you are is beyond even consciousness itself.

So, there's no point to getting wrapped up in kinesiology and making it a new obsessive-compulsive device to avoid reaching enlightenment. You don't have to calibrate everything on the planet. It is fun, however, and of course, we did it already. We did thousands. And we routinely do a thousand or two a year, just routinely. Just walking through the house, various things arise, partly because we get such an enormous amount of communication from all over, you know, all different countries around the clock, all different propositions, questions: "Would you go here, do this?" etc. The difficulty with physicality is that you're limited to the temporality of "here and now" with the physical self. Therefore, I never liked the physical self much, because it's an impediment. It's always in the way when you want to go someplace to do something. You've got to drag this around, and that can take hours a day, seeing as it's a drag. I just wanted to say, don't make kinesiology itself an obsession or a compulsion.

That which is necessary to know has already been spoken. It's already been shared; it's already been taught. It's the same throughout all of time. Anything that varies from that which has been taught throughout time is a variance from the truth. The truth is always the same. There's no variation from the truth. So, there's fancy side trips off into other domains and the lure of the siren's song, of specialness coming from various dimensions. These are all lures to pull you off the straight and narrow and test the conviction of your convictions. Don't allow yourself to be pulled off the central path.

POSE A QUESTION AS A MEDITATION

So, not all questions can be answered. Not all questions are necessary to answer. And many questions, what you do is, you pose them as a meditation, and you simply surrender them to God, see, because otherwise the ego just uses it as another way of maintaining its dominance over your consciousness—like, "I have to know if I had past lives or not." You don't have to know that. I mean, what has that got to do with totally surrendering to God, you know? It's helpful. So, a lot of these things are helpful to know at various places.

And it's a subtlety, a spiritual discernment to know when a thing is a distraction, or it's really significant and worthy of looking at.

Almost all things resolve themself by simply asking and then waiting. To simply ask, "What is the answer to this?" "What is the meaning of that?" "Does this pertain to me?" Then, the answer presents itself in due time. You see, we said the question here, and now we waited three minutes, and we ain't got an answer yet. "I'm waiting for the phone to ring, God!" When we ask a question, we mean like, "Right now," you know what I'm saying? Just know that it's heard, and when the time is appropriate—see, spiritual work is extremely subtle. The slightest move of an energy like this reveals an entire field like that that illuminates this entire landscape. It is not a linear "What is the answer to this?" question, and if I get the answer, then I am going to move from "here" to "there." It's more a way of *being* in the world. It's more of a contemplative way of being in the world. It's more a way of relating to the context of life and of your life, and of all of life, and of human life. It's more a way of relating to context than it is focusing on content. The content comes forth in due time.

So, the way to get an answer is to pose the question, meditate on it, turn it over to God, and ask God to help you understand, ask the Holy Spirit. You confess to the Holy Spirit; it doesn't seem to mind at all. "Why doesn't my ignition turn on? It's not turning on." The Holy Spirit is very helpful about such things. It seems to have a whole bunch of experts on the other side—electricians, mechanics, all kinds of people, map readers. I've found it very helpful. It doesn't have to be airy-fairy and sound very grandiose and very splendid in order to ask God a question, because the simplest things may be quite distressing. And you have to surrender your distress to God and ask for help with it.

We wanted to answer a few more questions. And what else were we going to say today? I just wanted to explain about the correspondence, about kinesiology. The other thing is about kinesiology because we get a lot of correspondence about that. I wish I'd never written about it. I'm like Galileo, that keeps getting letters about telescopes. He doesn't know anything about telescopes, you know. You put this glass here, you put this glass and look through here, and he says, "Wow, man, there's stars out there!" They keep writing me about telescopes. I don't know; there's experts that do kinesiology all day, every day, and it's their whole thing. And we try to send out a list of people we know who have demonstration tapes and explanations about it all. It's just a simple way of discerning the truth or falsehood of a single statement. It's nothing more than that. It's an assist; it's useful. Its primary use is really in doing research, the kind of research we did that went into *Power vs. Force*, etc., in getting answers to the unanswerable because they are outside of the linear domain. So, it's useful in exploring the realities of the nonlinear domain. If you're going to explore the linear domain, it's better to get a computer.

EXPLORING REALITIES IN THE NONLINEAR DOMAIN

[Q]: "Is it within God's wish for you to teach us all muscle testing today?"

That's hysterical! We do recapitulate this, because no matter how many tapes, videos, and lectures we give, for some reason some people are up against it with muscle testing. The reason they have a problem with it is because it's so simple. I find that things that are simple are very difficult to explain. I say, "Just put it here." Nobody gets that. "Just put it here." "What do you mean by 'here'?, 'when'?, 'now'?, 'this way?, or 'that'?" Of course, they've got to complicate everything—just put it here, man!

"It's *my* will to teach it." [True.] I did want to go over just. . . . People are getting calibrations that are too high, by virtue of the fact that they resist. It's a very fast, subtle energy.

"It's a very fast, subtle energy-resist." [True.] See, it's *very* quick. So, when I hold something negative in mind, it shoots down that fast. That's when you go weak. Then, the primate within us, the old primate out of evolution thinks it's falling out of a tree, and its antigravity muscles resist. See? We've noticed this all around the world. The minute the person goes weak, I say, "Hold bin Laden in mind." They start to go weak, and what happens then is they resist. You can't resist. It's very, very fast, so what you do is, you surrender. So, it's partly a willingness to surrender to weakness. Which sets the monkey in your unconscious into frantics, that he's going to fall out of the tree. So, you've got to retrain the monkey that he's okay to fall out of the tree. "Most people overly resist." [True.] "Therefore, they get calibrations that are way too high-resist." [True.] So, the thing is, you have to let go *instantly*. It's a subtlety. Anybody can totally resist, and you would never get a no, because no matter how hard you push, I can push harder, you understand? So, it's not a test of strength. It's a fast test—like that. Instantaneous test. "I'm holding something in mind-resist." [True.] "I'm holding something in mind-resist." [Not true.] The first time was Jesus Christ; the second time was bin Laden. You see how fast it went? Now, the other question that comes up is: Doesn't the other person's belief system affect the result? No, because she doesn't know what I was thinking. She has no belief system. She has no belief system about what I was thinking because she doesn't *know* what I was thinking.

Okay, the answer is very, very rapid. Consciousness *instantly* detects that which is deleterious to it and instantly detects that which is friendly to it. Extremely rapid, probably a 10th of a second. Let's see how fast it is; I never did measure it, come to think of it. "We have permission to measure this right here and now." [True.] "This discharge is longer than 1/100th of a second." [Not true.] "It's longer than 1/1,000th of a second." [Not true.] "It's 1/10,000th of a second." [True.] Approximately 1/10,000th of a second. So, it's something you "get" just by practice. It's more like, when you walk into a room, you've already "got" the energy of that room and the context of that room. It's very fast, very quick. With practice, you get it.

People who practice by themselves, with their middle finger and thumb together on one hand in the O-ring, are most prone to get high calibrations, because, again, you have to develop the sensitivity. And it's probably better to use the middle two fingers on one hand than these two fingers. These are very strong. If I make up my mind, it's going to be practically impossible to pull them apart, you understand? So, the tendency is to resist and

A New Paradigm of Reality

get calibrations that are way too high. These two fingers here do not have that much strength. Therefore, to use these two fingers here, the relative strength between truth and falsehood is much more easily perceived this way. As you know, trying to keep these two fingers apart, you really don't have much strength. If you try to keep these two fingers pressed together. Now, if I try to part them, you'll notice they are quite weak. I can't really part them, because they're very, very weak. So, using these two fingers here, the two middle fingers, is quicker and more sensitive because they are much weaker, and I can overpower them anytime, you see, because they don't have that much strength. So, you're not as likely to get a false positive.

Most things that are necessary to know, you know, have already been discussed and demonstrated. We are working on a book where we are doing a thousand calibrations. And as soon as we finish the book, *I*, this next one I've got halfway through. I'm trying to make a reference book because lots of people have many questions, and they can't really do it themselves, or they don't have a partner they can do it with. And it will be sort of easy to be able to look up very spiritual authors in history—what level of consciousness? The levels of consciousness are not "better than." The ego tends to think of "better than" or "less than." There are many terrific teachers in the high 200s. I mean, the basics of spirituality, you don't have to be a rocket scientist. To be kind, loving, forgiving, unselfish, to be of service to others, to see the value of worship and prayer and dedication of surrendering all one's service and efforts to God. To stop looking for rewards in the world and do them for their own sake, out of one's love for God and one's fellow man. Those things are very simple and also very difficult, as we all know. And it takes years of practice before one goes on and needs more advanced spiritual techniques.

As we've said, salvation is one thing, enlightenment is another. Enlightenment is far more demanding, more strict, more radical. Radical. You've got to be actually willing to get riddled with bullets if that's what it takes to walk beyond identifying yourself as a physical body and giving in and giving power to fear. So, it's extremely radical to reach enlightenment; it's extremely demanding, and you can be asked to give up anything, and you have to be willing to surrender anything and everything.

When I said, if that music puts you in that very unique, divine space, then I would just stay in that space. I would never do anything but play the music, month after month after month, year after year—until one's finally willing to do it forever. Instantly, you're into that forever. So, those which are great gains sometimes require great commitments and great sacrifices. So, when one reaches a certain state, one will like, know it; like one is almost compelled to leave everything and devote oneself to a very intense spirituality, and that's the call and you say yes to it. And then you *go* for it. And you make what I call "the run." You make the "final run," where nothing stops you, nothing gets in your way. You sacrifice and surrender anything and everything that stands in the way: the willingness to leave the world and everything in it. The titles, the riches, the family members, whatever it takes—you walk out, walk away—whatever you have to do, you have to do. So, those are the things that come up later, not this morning. You don't have to leave your car and take the bus today.

[Q]: *"The collective consciousness—what is the effect of the terrorist attacks?"*

I think the effect of the terrorist attacks is actually to elevate the consciousness. I think, following that, we all became more spiritual, more committed to integrity, more to questioning. Go over the moral agonizing of what should be the response to it. What does it mean to be patriotic? Should we have "In God We Trust" on our money? I always think that's so funny. It's our money. "In God We Trust" on a dollar bill: I mean, there's God and money, you know. Which is more important? It's hard to say, isn't it? Should we take "God" off of the money? What should one's relationship to one's country be, and to what degree, and in what context? So, I think there's a great deal of benefit to the country. There's a real live wakening to the reality of spiritual and theological questions. And, unfortunately, those who do the voting and talking most of the

A New Paradigm of Reality

time don't know the difference between religion and spirituality. That's the difficulty, isn't it? The difficulty is they don't understand the Constitution.

To get elected to Congress, you don't have to understand the Constitution. I myself would make them all pass a test of whether they understand the Constitution of the United States before they swear to uphold it. You don't know the difference between religion and spirituality. The Constitution of the United States calibrates in the 700s. It says that: by virtue of the Divinity of our origin, that is the source of our equality. And, out of that equality, then, we acknowledge God as our Source, and out of acknowledging our God as Source, therefore we establish no religion. Because of the powerful truth of spirituality, the state shall establish no religion. And, in enforcing the Spiritual Truth, then, it guarantees the freedom of religion, because the government shall neither prohibit nor establish a religion. In other words, the government, because its Source is Spiritual Truth, keeps its hand off all religions. So, the word *God* is merely a word, and to say, to reiterate the source of the power of the Constitution, does not establish religion. So, the objection to it was—first of all, it does not say in it that—the political opposition to it was confusing that the government shall not establish a religion. So, to mention the word *God* as the Source of man's origin is not a religion. That is not a religion.

So, one is free to talk about Satan in colleges; the colleges established the Satan club. Could you believe a "Satan club"? And it goes along with the music we hear in MTV and all. I guess that's the music that goes with the Satan club. It's an odd paradox that it's okay to establish a Satan club, but it is not okay to mention God, so that's a peculiar perversion of Truth, which is based on a Luciferic energy. The Luciferic likes to turn things into their opposites, so that you become the defender of evil in the name of Truth. When bin Laden's last days arise, you can be sure they'll all be out there with the placards: "Bin Laden's rights are being violated!" Forget that 3,000 people and their families and all the rest of us. . . . So that confusion of Truth, then—the Luciferic energy tries to reverse good and evil and make them look like their opposites. So, I think that our country is looking at that, you know? It's confronted with: What is religion? What is spirituality? What is integrity? What is truth? What is our commitment? What is the difference between nationalism and patriotism? People don't even get that. They discuss it, and they don't even know the difference, because nationalism is "bad"; therefore, we should not be patriotic. That's confusing two things altogether; they are two different domains. Patriotism comes from the heart. Nationalism is a political control technique, you know. They are not the same thing. So, there's big mistakes made just due to ignorance, of not knowing the difference between religion and spirituality, not knowing the difference between patriotism and nationalism.

In Nazi Germany, we see the apex of nationalism, "Deutschland Uber Alles," and its appeal. So, you can see how people would later mistrust that. Patriotism is love for one's country. When you love your country, it doesn't have to dominate anybody else. We don't see America invading Canada, invading Mexico, taking over the Caribbean. See what I am saying? It's sufficient unto itself. To love one's country is to love one's fellow man.

"As far as walk-ins and soul-exchangers, that's an illusion-resist." [True.] Yes, that's an illusion. That's some kind of a pop spirituality concept that there's "walk-ins," and then there are people with their tailbones missing, and they are all looking for specialness. It's all looking for specialness. One doesn't need to be special. See, when you surrender all to God, humility means there's no need to be special. There's no need for recognition. There's no need for titles, possessions, control, doesn't want followers, money, doesn't have to have membership; people don't have to sign up; they don't have to be a member of the club, don't have to go through initiation. They don't put a rattlesnake in your mailbox if you decide to leave.

No, spirituality means freedom, to be where you want to be for the benefit of being there, because the karmic merit is your own decision to be there for its own sake. If you're going to church because you'll go to hell if you don't go to church, what is the karmic merit in that? Spiritual growth comes from saying yes to that

A New Paradigm of Reality

which is positive, seeking that which you feel is beneficial, and not avoiding the negative, but choosing the positive. The way out of the duality of good and evil, and good and bad, is to choose the good, choose the positive. There's no point in battling "evil," because then you just give it some kind of reality, an energy of reality. No, what you do is choose . . . the way out of that one is you merely choose the good, you might say. Choose Truth over falsehood.

Ah, well, it's true that with kinesiology and with karmic research, you can discover the source of a lot of things. Now, there are a lot of people that write books on past-life research; I don't know all their names, but they are specialists in it, and there are various techniques. There are simple hypnotic techniques where you count back, and you go to a certain time. And you come up the elevator and step out, and the whole panorama begins to present itself. And with that, there's often a recognition—a lot of times, you suddenly remember it; if it's valid, you'll remember it. It's not just a recall in sort of a trance state. You, frankly, remember it, and you remember the circumstances. Sometimes, you wish you didn't. You remember the circumstances. And that may start a chain of them in which you can remember quite a few lifetimes. Without much difficulty, you can remember quite a few lifetimes. And then, at a certain level of consciousness, because you don't identify with this physicality, you identify more with the evolution of consciousness back through time. And then there's the recall and awareness of all kinds of lifetimes, and usually, with an awareness of what the purpose of that encounter was.

[Q]: "Can you find out Spiritual Truths for a third person?"

Yes, you can do that. And a lot of times, you know we do it on behalf of someone else, at their request, because they don't have a partner to do it, etc. They'll say, "Could you ask this or that for me?" So, there, you have to get karmic permission. You have to get their permission, and you also have to ask. Sometimes it's merely a way of the person's bypassing facing a spiritual past that they've got to handle with themselves, you know. Sometimes kinesiology can be

KARMA AND DEVOTION

used more to escape spiritual responsibility, rather than actually advance your own consciousness.

[Q]: "What does it mean when you think you are making progress in your spiritual work, and all of a sudden it all goes down the drain? Everything is in chaos, and all the garbage of your life comes out?"

Oh, it means you are making fantastic progress. When you're BS'ing around in your head and thinking you're doing spirituality, nothing really happens. When you get serious about it, all kinds of stuff can come out of the woodwork. And that's quite true. So, the lives of spiritual seekers are often quite turbulent.

The calibration of various spiritual teachers is somewhat difficult to explain. Many people, spiritual teachers and otherwise, calibrate quite high; they do very good work in the world. They attain recognition, power, financial gain, etc. Elected president of the country. And then—and then—they crash. Then it goes to their head, you might say, the Luciferic energy of power, money, control. So, we see a lot of people . . . there's gurus that write books that are usually in the high 500s and gain a lot of followers, then somehow, the ego gets pulled into it and they succumb to the glamour of all that. And then you see that suddenly their calibration goes way down. The book they wrote in the 500s may still be in the 500s. They, as a person, as an entity right now, may calibrate quite low. It happened with Napoleon. It happened with Hitler.

"We have permission to do Napoleon-resist." [True.] "Napoleon on his rise was over 450." [True.] "460." [True.] "470." [True.] "480." [Not true.] He was a brilliant man. He calibrates at 480—that's very high intelligence. He was probably a very brilliant military strategist. Napoleon—okay. "Later, before he died, Napoleon calibrated over 200-resist." [Not true.] Napoleon was 480; that's really way up there. And then, somehow being emperor, being commander . . . maybe the accumulated karma of killing many innocent people—oh, that could be it.

"We have permission to ask about Adolph Hitler." [True.] "When he wrote *Mein Kampf*, was over 400." [True.] "450." [Not

A New Paradigm of Reality

true.] "440." [True.] "445." [Not true.] So, Hitler was a politician; he stood for national socialism. And he wrote his political treatise in prison and after the push failed; he was over 450 at the time. "Before he died, Adolph Hitler was over 200-resist." [Not true.] I don't want to tell you how low he was. So, you see, it's not just gurus.

A person like that will retain the image of what they were when they were in their higher state, and people relate to that image. Even at the end of the war, I'm sure there were a lot of people that believed in Hitler. They believed in him still, even though he led the country down to disaster and destruction. The destruction of Cologne, I mean, the beautiful cities, Dresden—the incredible beauty that was destroyed in the name of war; that, in itself must have a bad karmic consequence, to destroy so much beauty. But I'm sure there were still people that believed in him. The image may outlast the reality. The image outlasts the reality. What the person *was* is still being glorified or respected, and they don't see what the person is now; they only see what the person was at their highest level of functioning, umm. So, it happens even to military commanders, and it happens to politicians all the time, and celebrities of course.

It happens to celebrities once they get in the eye of popularity and all the paparazzi are after them, etc. It's very hard for them not to crash. I feel sorry for them. And, of course, many great rock stars and all, we saw them start out humbly and full of joy, and then end up crashing and committing suicide and dying of drugs, etc. So, to take that onslaught of popularity and the media, the spotlight of the media, money, prestige, followers. You can imagine putting on a concert—what do they have, like 10,000 people out there? Thirty thousand or something? It must be staggering for their ego to handle that and not become grandiose and sucked in by the glamour, sucked in by the glamour of it.

So, one of the great seducers then, is glamour. "One of the great seducers is glamour-resist." [True.] "The glamour of success." [True.] "The glamour of prestige." [True.] Oh, yeah, it isn't just the prestige and the power; it's the *glamour* of it. There was, I think, a

KARMA AND DEVOTION

book written about glamour as a specific energy, written by Alice Bailey. "Glamour—we have permission to ask that." [True.] "Is a specific energy-resist." [True.] Yes, it is a specific energy. So, that's an interesting thing to know, that certain accomplishments then will attract that energy of glamour, which itself could lead to your downfall. You become captured by that. "So, one becomes captured by that energy of glamour." [True.] "Seduced by it-resist." [True.] "Captivated by it." [True.] Oh. "And enslaved by it." [True.] Uh-oh, one becomes enslaved by it. Uh-oh. So, that would explain then, the fall of many—the glamour.

Gratitude is one of the most wonderful things and helpful spiritually. "Gratitude is over 500-resist." [True.] "510." [True.] "520." [True.] "530." [Not true.] 520, 530. It's the way of the heart. Gratitude is a way of the heart—thankfulness and gratitude, and it's very important in many spiritual pathways. It is certainly in the 12-step programs—it's a very, very big piece of the program. Instead of resentments, you're grateful for what you have. The way of the heart, then. Twelve-step groups are a way of the heart, a way of surrendering. And, through the third step, one surrenders one's will to God and is grateful for all experiences, because, as someone said to me the other day, "You get the experiences that you need." You can't get from "here" to "there" without going through "here." You understand? So that would explain why the world appears as it does, because it requires, to grow spiritually, many opportunities, which this world provides. This world . . . in other words, if you were in a beautiful monastery where everybody is unconditionally loving and you do nothing but listen to birds and garden all day, there's a limited amount of karmic possibilities there, correct? Give up sex, maybe, okay. Seventy-five years in a monastery, and out of that lifetime, you learn to let sex go. Yeah. "I could be *happy* without sex." Okay. If you can do that one in one lifetime, that's pretty good. Now, in the world which most of us live, the opportunities are complex, multitudinous, and constantly presenting themself. So, if you want to evolve rapidly, it seems to me this world would be the ideal place. This is a wonderful place. All you have to do is turn on the TV, you've got an opportunity to let go of hate, let go of fear, let go of greed, let go of lust, avarice, as they shake on the screen and invite you to "try this," which will turn you into more of a man or your money back. I mean, the seductions on the presentations. And the latest person to hate and the latest person to fear, the latest political shenanigan to twist your mind with. The appeal to all the vanities, to appearance, to glamour—it's just an endless barrage. So, if you have to pick a world for rapid spiritual evolution, I think this is the ultimate. "That's true-resist." [True.] "This is almost the ultimate opportunity-resist." [True.] "And that's why it's a gift to be born a human." [True.] "Which is what the Buddha meant-resist." [True.] Aha! So, the Buddha was right to say *it's a great gift to be born a human, because it opens the chance to evolve all the way to enlightenment, just in one lifetime.*

CLOSING PRAYER

We are grateful to be here. We're grateful to be here, O Lord. We give thanks for this world and the multitudinous opportunities it presents, and prayerfully, we are grateful and thankful for this lifetime.

Conclusion

We hope after reading this book, walking the Pathway of Love is a much closer reality than what you may have thought. Dr. Hawkins in his devotion and dedication, reassures us that we have within us the capacity to "Be the prayer." A person can choose compassion over judgment, live with care instead of malice, and feel gratitude for life's challenges, having the deeper understanding that life experiences can bring the greatest spiritual growth and the opportunity to be forgiving and kind hearted.

As Dr. Hawkins said, people are more loving than they realize. It may be expressed as duty, commitment, caringness, and even love for the body. In its spiritual form, it is an awareness of a reality that is within you at all times. At a certain point, a person sees love everywhere; it is a constant in our lives, and he invites us to nurture those parts of ourselves.

To gain deeper insights, read this book often or watch or listen to the September and October 2002 lectures that are available. Just receiving the information itself can be transformative and awe-inspiring in an instant!

The following are some of the Spiritual Truths in this volume that a person can contemplate as they go through their day:

- "Love is a Way of Being in the World."
- "Love is actually a style. . . . It is a way of holding yourself in life and every aspect of life within an overall context, which gives it a different meaning and significance.
- Inner Renunciation—the willingness to let go of everything that stands in the way of Love.

- Ask the question, "Am I willing to surrender that to God? Would I rather be right or would I rather realize the Presence of God?
- Spiritual work is really the willingness to surrender all the blocks to Love.
- Spiritual work is a form of Love.
- Out of compassion for yourself, you are willing to let go of the things that bring you pain, suffering, guilt. "I am not going to allow myself to fall into the pit."
- The Pathway of Love is sanctifying all of your life in all of its details and all its expressions as an expression or love for God and to all that exists.
- What is the significance of karma? It has the capacity to light up areas of your own life so that they make sense.
- One gets a chance to undo the negative karma." [True.] "And acquire positive karma." [True.]
- Some comprehension of the nature of karma and maybe how it came about in your own lifetime can facilitate certain difficult things to transcend.
- Special Prayer: "Out of love for Thee, Oh Lord, I let go of my attachment to so-an-so. I surrender it to Thee."

Here is a helpful question that was asked in this volume:

"How can we surrender everything to God?"

The willingness to surrender to God is sort of a catch-22 because there is a love for God that is so deep within yourself, so profound, so exquisitely intense, that, for God, one would surrender anything. It's something to be discovered. It's there; that capacity, that willingness to surrender everything to God is innate within consciousness. When you need it and call it forth, it's there. Would I be willing to surrender "this" to God? Yes.

Conclusion

Straight and Narrow is the Path . . . Waste No Time.

Gloria in Excelsis Deo!

About the Author

David R. Hawkins, M.D., Ph.D. (1927–2012), was director of The Institute for Spiritual Research, Inc., and founder of the Path of Devotional Nonduality. He was renowned as a pioneering researcher in the field of consciousness as well as an author, lecturer, clinician, physician, and scientist. He served as an advisor to Catholic and Protestant churches, and Buddhist monasteries; appeared on major network television and radio programs; and lectured widely at such places as Westminster Abbey, the Oxford Forum, the University of Notre Dame, and Harvard University. His life was devoted to the upliftment of mankind until his death in 2012.

veritaspub.com

Hay House Titles of Related Interest

YOU CAN HEAL YOUR LIFE, the movie,
starring Louise Hay & Friends
(available as an online streaming video)
www.hayhouse.co.uk/louise-movie

THE SHIFT, the movie,
starring Dr Wayne W. Dyer
(available as an online streaming video)
www.hayhouse.co.uk/the-shift-movie

***

THE AWAKENED WAY: Making the Shift to a Divinely Guided Life
by Suzanne Giesemann

THE BIOLOGY OF BELIEF: Unleashing the Power of Consciousness, Matter & Miracles by Bruce H. Lipton, PhD

CONSCIOUSNESS IS ALL THERE IS: How Understanding and Experiencing Consciousness Will Transform Your Life by Dr Tony Nader

INTENTIONALITY: A Groundbreaking Guide to Breath, Consciousness and Radical Self-Transformation by Finnian Kelly

PURE HUMAN: The Hidden Truth of Our Divinity, Power and Destiny
by Gregg Braden

All of the above are available at your local bookstore,
or may be ordered by contacting Hay House (see next page).

***

We hope you enjoyed this Hay House book. If you'd like to receive our online catalogue featuring additional information on Hay House books and products, please contact:

Hay House UK Ltd
1st Floor, Crawford Corner,
91–93 Baker Street, London W1U 6QQ
Tel: +44 (0)20 3927 7290; www.hayhouse.co.uk

———

Published in the United States of America by:
Hay House LLC
PO Box 5100, Carlsbad, CA 92018-5100
Tel: (760) 431-7695 or (800) 654-5126
www.hayhouse.com

Published in Australia by:
Hay House Australia Publishing Pty Ltd
18/36 Ralph St., Alexandria NSW 2015
Tel: +61 (02) 9669 4299
www.hayhouse.com.au

Published in India by:
Hay House Publishers (India) Pvt Ltd
Muskaan Complex, Plot No. 3,
B-2, Vasant Kunj, New Delhi 110 070
Tel: +91 11 41761620
www.hayhouse.co.in

———

Let Your Soul Grow

Experience life-changing transformation – one video at a time – with guidance from the world's leading experts.

www.healyourlifeplus.com

TRANSFORM YOUR DAY—ANYTIME, ANYWHERE

With the **Empower You** Unlimited Audio *App*

> 66 ★★★★★ **Life changing.**
> My fav app on my entire phone, hands down! – Gigi 99

Unlimited access to the entire Hay House audio library!

You'll get:

- 600+ soul-stirring **audiobooks** to expand your mind
- 1,000+ **meditations** for restful sleep, morning focus, and gentle healing
- Bite-sized audios **under 20 minutes**—perfect for busy days
- **Exclusive talks** you won't find anywhere else
- **Daily affirmations**
- Fresh content added **every week** to fuel your journey

New audios added every week!

> 66 Driving, yard work, and housework have been **transformed!**
> – Ruffles27 99

Scan the QR code to start listening or visit **hayhouse.com/unlimited**

HAY HOUSE
Online Video Courses

Your journey to a better life starts with figuring out which path is best for you. Hay House Online Courses provide guidance in mental and physical health, personal finance, telling your unique story, and so much more!

LEARN HOW TO:

- choose your words and actions wisely so you can tap into life's magic
- clear the energy in yourself and your environments for improved clarity, peace, and joy
- forgive, visualize, and trust in order to create a life of authenticity and abundance
- manifest lifelong health by improving nutrition, reducing stress, improving sleep, and more
- create your own unique angelic communication toolkit to help you to receive clear messages for yourself and others
- use the creative power of the quantum realm to create health and well-being

To find the guide for your journey, visit www.HayHouseU.com.

HAY HOUSE
online learning

CONNECT WITH
HAY HOUSE
ONLINE

🌐 hayhouse.co.uk f @hayhouse

📷 @hayhouseuk 🦋 @hayhouseuk.bsky.social

♪ @hayhouseuk ▶ @HayHousePresents

> Find out all about our latest books & card decks • Be the first to know about exclusive discounts • Interact with our authors in live broadcasts • Celebrate the cycle of the seasons with us • Watch free videos from your favourite authors • Connect with like-minded souls

'The gateways to wisdom and knowledge are always open.'

Louise Hay